The Red Gown

Love, a Dress Rehearsal?

By Cynthia M. Long

This account is based on a true story. I have tried to recreate events, locales, and conversations from memories of them. In order to maintain anonymity in some instances, I have changed the names of individuals and some identifying characteristics of a few events.

In Gratitude

To my wonderful children. In appreciation for all your assistance these last few years, especially during the most difficult moments in my life. Thank you for deeply caring and assisting. Love you forever.

To my son-in-law. Thank you for all your assistance. Very much appreciated.

To my sweetheart. I'm grateful for you showing up at a time I had no interest in a relationship. You didn't give up! Thank you for standing in the middle of the fire with me, even when it was difficult. This affirms your commitment and true love.

To my three charming grandsons… May you not lose the unconditional love you arrived with. Humanity's truest teachers of love are our little ones.

To my friends who have been patient with all the wildness in my life… I'm thankful for your friendship and assistance, especially during trying times.

I'm grateful for the challenges, some small, others not so small. Though I'm worn, it definitely assisted in helping stretch and grow, so I could ultimately become a better person. They say God doesn't give too much to handle. There were times I disagreed.

Bless all for support, patience, and love during the "what the OM is going on!

Contents

1: Everything Starts with a Beginning

San Paulo, Brazil Airport—January 2001

I was contemplating the long flight home to the Bay Area in California after a month's stay in the mystical country of Brazil, the land of my grandfather's family heritage. He was the grandfather that I never knew. Then again, my mother, his youngest daughter, really never knew him either. My immigrant grandfather, Manuel Alfonso Jardim, could have been the inventor of the improved automatic windshield wiper if he hadn't been mugged one early spring day in the 1930s, beaten to a pulp, severely brain damaged—his precious plans and dreams ripped out of his hands. This tragedy occurred while he was on his way to Ford Motor Company for a special meeting. My grandfather was lost on the streets for several months, not knowing who or where he was. Eventually he was found and was admitted to a mental hospital, but his life was never the same again. Manuel was a victim of a crime that was never resolved legally or within the family system. His future was stolen and his family forever scarred by the horrific nightmare—or was it?

My Portuguese grandmother, Avozinha (which means young grandmother), and five her children left my grandfather a few years after his mugging. Heading to California from Massachusetts by Greyhound, my grandmother could only afford to send her eldest two twenty-something young-adult children first. Uncle Oscar and Aunt Lydia were very excited about the move to California in one sense. In another, they were uncertain, feeling pulled by the recurring thoughts of abandoning their father. Yet they witnessed the daily struggles their mother endured to provide for them and their siblings. They were also tired of the very cold winters in Massachusetts and welcomed the calmer climate in California where their grandmother and great-grand-mother lived. The two teen children were sent next. My cautious Aunt Mary had to keep an eye on my adventurous and rambunctious Uncle Al as he would frequently wander off at bus stops to explore new territory. The bus almost left without them a few times. Aunt Mary was quite anxious throughout the lengthy bus ride, just to be free of the responsibility.

Avozinha and my four-year-old mother, Nueme, arrived last. My mother doesn't remember much except that it was a long and bumpy ride, and she had motion sickness a great deal during the journey. Two-by-two, they aimed for the land of opportunity and rarely looked back. Perhaps Avozinha needed the closeness of her birth family since she had no other relatives. Or perhaps she had enough of all the trials and tribulations the East Coast afforded. Raising five children alone, thousands of miles away from the only family she had, would have been a daunting task.

Avozinha was a stoic woman with a hardened smile, which I believe hid many painful sorrows behind the seemingly built-in disguise. She grew up in privilege in Portugal, on the island of Funchal. Avozinha spoke five languages and was a gourmet cook and baker. A seamstress extraordinaire, she knitted and crocheted creative works throughout her life. If I ever wanted a dress made, I would show Avozinha a photo, she would observe the angles carefully, draw the image, cut the pattern from day-old newspaper, and whip it up with ease on her old-fashioned pedaled sewing machine. Perhaps this was her therapy, a mantra of repetition, like a meditation—each colorful stitch held together a piece of art that was part of the love she couldn't express easily in words or affection.

Avozinha arrived with her mother on Ellis Island in New York at age thirteen after living with her godmother in Portugal. For most of her young life, Avozinha thought that this woman, whom she adored, was her mother. Unfortunately, one very emotional day, her godmother died unexpectedly. Avozinha was torn away from that life of privilege and told she was moving to the United States with a woman she later discovered was her birth mother.

Details about her real father's life remained vague until some of our family traveled to Funchal, Portugal, several years later and sought out a genealogist during our visit. His findings were startling. My grandmother was a product of a love affair between my great-grandmother and a wealthy, married business man. Perhaps Avozinha's identity had to remain hidden until it was certain she would be leaving Funchal. And maybe this was why her godmother raised her.

A few of us in our family who have taken interest in genealogy feel the alleged father secretively paid for Avozinha's birth mother's passage to America. All the other details of this affair were buried with Avozinha, except the few pieces we found and her supposed father's signature on the Ellis Island arrival documents.

At fifteen years of age, Avozinha entered into an arranged marriage with my grandfather, a promising business man. She never thought her life would end up full of twists and turns, in a maze of turmoil and sacrifice. Laborious and back-breaking factory work after the prosperous and happy years helped mold Avozinha's impassive silhouette, one that lightened after a second marriage while in her sixties.

Interestingly, there was never a word spoken about my grandfather from my grandmother's lips. And not one thing was mentioned from our mother about our grandfather. As we got older and more curious, a few of us asked our elder uncles questions about our grandparents' lives. Our uncles related age-perspective points of view. The oldest uncle knew much more and took a mature approach since he was nine years older than his brother. Each freely told stories of our grandparents' two successful businesses. The tone changed with both uncles when the subject surfaced concerning the stressful years during the stock market crash. It was difficult to hear that our grandparents lost everything, but it was a common occurrence during that era. Maybe the last sorrow in Massachusetts was more than my grandmother could deal with. We will never know.

My Brazilian immigrant grandfather drank a lot after the crash, and that was a problem for the family. I was told that he was a true entrepreneur—a dreamer with his head in the clouds. He always found unique ways of making a living until that fateful day, with hopeful plans in hand, and possibly a strong belief of a fresh new start for his loved ones and himself. This misfortune changed the course of an entire family's life forever.

If my grandfather's invention had been purchased by Ford, I wondered about the "what if's." If my grandmother had stayed married, lived in Massachusetts, and raised her children there, my mother would not have met my father, and my siblings and I wouldn't have been born. Then this story would have never occurred. Is this what fate and destiny are about? Is fate different from destiny?

Because Avozinha took most of this story and others to her grave, it's been a hit-and-miss search for more information. Through the years, lost pieces have come together. Most of my immigrant grandfather's background was a mystery. He spent the rest of his life in a care home, alone. Some years back, I tried to locate his birth family in Brazil.

I had an interest in genealogy then, but life got very busy and somewhat complicated, so I put the sparse information I'd gathered away. Sadly enough, it's been stored for almost two decades.

These recollections of my family history have come in and out of my memory over the years, but never as strongly as the moment I placed my own feet on Brazilian soil. I surprisingly had a sense of homecoming in Brazil, a place I felt I belonged. I first thought the journey was meant to learn about ancient healing practices and catch up on much-needed rest from a very busy schedule. But my opinion changed dramatically: I now felt connected in such a compelling way that it was difficult to explain.

Returning to the moment, I was on the edge of my seat at the airport in San Paulo, Brazil, since I was on standby. My daughter worked for a major airline and, as part of the perks, parents were able to fly for free on standby passes. I used these passes once in awhile and felt blessed, unless I was stuck in an airport somewhere. If seats sold out, I would wait for the next flight and hope there was an empty seat available. There were occasions when I had to spend hours upon hours at the airport, or even overnight. The wait at the airport that day was not an easy one. I had to remind myself to trust that I'd be taken care of and relax into the experience.

At one point I questioned whether I would get out of San Paulo since the flight was overbooked. I feared spending the night in a city harboring eight million people without knowing their language. My system was shocked after being in a serene love bubble, a secluded Shangri-La of sorts, at the healing center of Abadiania, a community like no other. A place I was able to rest, regroup, and heal. A magical place that worked on a person from the inside out. This community somehow assisted in a shift in one's perception of the world and, at one crucial point, one's belief system.

Being a middle-aged woman who rarely ventured this far from of my comfort zone, the thought of getting stranded made me a bit uneasy. I prayed intently. As I watched the passengers load onto the airbus, I went up to the podium once more. As I approached the attendant, she asked me to stand close by. I took a few deep breaths as I eyed the bus filled with people. I silently asked in prayer, once again, for assistance and patience. I glanced meekly at the attendant; she smiled and said with a Brazilian accent, "You're a lucky woman today! Someone didn't show up!" I wanted to jump up and down for joy like a child, but I held it together. She handed me my ticket. I smiled, thanked her, and rushed out of the door, tugging my carry-on behind. I entered the over-crowded bus and off we went. I immediately searched the ticket for the seat assignment; it was a low number, which usually meant first class.

2: John of God and Healing

The ride home was comfortable and much appreciated. I felt like an empress returning from a long relaxing holiday! Every need was taken care of with manners and grace. My meal was presented like a prop for a gourmet magazine. It was delicious. I rested, read, and reminisced. We landed in San Francisco without an issue. I called my sister to inform her that I would be in front of the international arrival area for pickup. I scooped up my luggage and waited at the curb.

I was in such a daze from the month long journey at the spiritual community in Abadiania, Brazil, and only half paying attention to the cars passing by, feeling ungrounded and somewhat scattered from all the people, noise, and general racket—so much buzzing around in every direction. I was now highly sensitive to all the noise pollution. It felt uncomfortable and unnatural. I then noticed my sister and my mother, and waved as they approached. June, my sister, got out and helped load my large bags in her car, and then we drove away.

"So, tell us…how was it?" June and my mother asked excitedly as they peered over the back where I was sitting. Their anxious faces made me smile.

My mother and sister were all ears for news about my trip.

"I don't know where to begin. It was an experience not many would understand. Honestly, I didn't want to leave."

I paused.

"I witnessed incredible healings there! People rolled in by the busloads from all over the world. Some even traveled on foot from the remote areas of Brazil. The miracles totally blew my mind! It would take hours to explain it all to you. One needs be there to fully understand John of God's gifts and what goes on at this unassuming community."

Not one peep out of my sister and mother.

I continued, "I'm going to share something unbelievable. Are you ready?"

They both half turned to look at me, then at each other and smiled. It felt like they were not certain and only smiled because it was a polite thing to do.

"John of God uses a common kitchen knife and no anesthesia to remove a tumor from an individual's body. There's virtually no blood. Incisions close and heal instantly. Very few could comprehend what he does unless they saw it with their own eyes. This is not anything the mainstream populous could even imagine! Most would assume it's a scam."

I caught my sister's gaze in the rearview mirror.

"What?" She was mind-boggled, but totally trusted what I had just communicated.

I took a deep breath while still focusing on my sister. I was all wound up, reviewing what had just come pouring out of my mouth.

"Are you kidding?" June replied in an excited voice. "Wow! There's no anesthesia? What do they do about the pain?"

June was staring at me off and on from the mirror while she drove through the busy traffic maze. My mother remained very quiet. I sat there filling my lungs for the next round of information.

"Sometimes there is some discomfort, but most often it subsides on the spot. Everyone I witnessed could tolerate the pain after their surgery. It sounds fabricated, I'm sure. But I've heard no mention of infections or complications in any of the thousands upon thousands of people John of God has attended in the last forty years. He just sits or stands in front of the person and scans them without touching. When it was my turn, he examined me and told the translator in Portuguese what I needed to do. In my case, I was to go to a certain area of The Casa."

June butted in, "Cin, what do you mean, he sits or stands before the people he heals?"

"Just what I said. He appears to be in this trance state and can literally look through a person's body to see where the problem lies."

"That is unreal, Cin! I've never heard of anything like that before!" June shook her head trying to comprehend the magnitude of this information.

My mother turned to listen more intently.

"And what's *The Casa*?" June asked curiously.

"The Casa is the facility where all healing takes place. The way this center works, it takes a team to set the stage, so to speak, for the healing process to begin. There are six areas in this center. After being briefed, I started moving toward one of the rooms to meditate. This room was called *The Current Room* and dedicated to meditation. Those who entered The Current Room were prepared energetically. Before sitting to meditate, I observed the people in white, and the various framed photographs and paintings on the wall. Some were religious, Catholic influence since Brazil has a large Catholic following, others of world master teachers, and those of the entities John of God incorporates. An interesting thing I noticed that this center welcomed all people, not just Catholics. That's how it should be."

June and my mother nodded in agreement.

"Cin, why is the one area called *The Current Room*?" June was full of questions.

"The Current Room is filled with meditators, which bring the healing vibration to a level where healing is possible. Again, it's truly a group effort."

"Healing vibration? Sounds *woo woo*." June laughed.

"I guess some may have this belief, but what I witnessed, so did thousands of others before me. There was no doubt. Much has been kept from the mainstream. It's probably considered outdated, but mainly because it's free. This healing method has been around for eons.

"There were a few people there that had only one week to live according to traditional medicine. But they were completely healed. One woman had Lupus. Her doctors forbid her from traveling since the Lupus was in her brain and she could die in flight. She was dependent upon a wheelchair. Her partner was desperate. He chose to ignore the doctors and risked taking her on this long trip anyway. She was on tons of medications, which added to her dire health dilemma. When the woman was wheeled in front of John of God, he told the translator, in Portuguese, she had to stay at least three months to heal completely. In three months, indeed, a miracle occurred. She was off all the medications and jogging again. I witnessed the first month of her healing.

"So, John of God doesn't speak English? June asks.

"No. Another man was in a wheelchair for some degenerative disease. He was very ill. I got to see him walk again. He was told he was cured, and it certainly looked that way."

"Wow!" My mother joined in this time. "Cin, I'm having difficulty hearing that someone who is wheelchair-bound can walk in an instant? And those who are on their deathbeds are also cured. How is this humanly possible? And does everyone get cured?"

I replied, "Everyone receives a healing, not everyone is cured. I guess a cure is called a miracle. And there have been many there. There's an outside room dedicated to all the wheelchairs, crutches, and whatever else people leave behind. I was told that those who are not cured still have things to clear up within themselves. And anyone associated with someone ill has signed up for this challenging lesson to also learn and grow. Often it's not the same lesson with those who are ill. There are some individuals who John of God tells to go home and prepare for death—that their time is up on this planet. This is most difficult for those not ready to die.

"One of my posada neighbors had cervical cancer and returned to Abadiania for the third visit in great hope of getting cured. She was in remission for many years, but her cancer returned with a vengeance as it spread throughout her body. She confided in me one early morning while I was sitting outside my room reading. She was told to go home and prepare for transition. She was very distressed considering her child was still a young teen. I was able to be there for her during this poignant moment as she began to accept the fears she had. This is when believing in heaven is put to the test in a big way."

June was extremely quiet since she had a few close friends that had just passed away from cancer. My mother jumped in with a non-threatening tone.

"What do you mean by *entities John of God incorporates*?" My mother asked in a questioning manner.

"And why do people wear white?" My sister curiously added.

I replied, "First, there's something about white clothing. In preparing for my trip, there was a list of things I was told to bring. And on the list was white clothing. I remembered this was a common practice throughout history and even today. In Catholicism, white is worn in baptism, First Communion, and marriage. The Missionaries of Charity, Mother Theresa's order wear white with a bit of blue. In India, many teachers and gurus wear white. Some say it is a color for wisdom and purity. I feel it's a color that helps the healing process."

I observed that my mother was still very eager to hear the answer to her own question, so I replied, "So, to answer your question, Mother, to surely give John of God due respect, I need to at least provide some background history before I tell you about the entities. It's a bit of a story if you are willing to hear it?" I asked.

"We have an hour!" my sister said. With a fixed stare, my mother gave a half smile.

"John of God's given name is Joao. It's been stated he was born in central Brazil and lived in poverty as a child. He had little formal education, but Joao was born clairvoyant with incredible abilities, and this started his life's work for the healing mission. Joao left home on foot as a teen to work as a tailor, but it lasted only one day. He was miles away from family and had no money, even for food. He was distressed, not knowing where his next meal would come from. Can you imagine?"

"I cannot imagine," my sister responded.

"Today, there's still such poverty. We don't hear about this much unless one is well-traveled or well-read," I added.

"So, Joao decided to forget about the disturbing feelings and went swimming in a nearby creek. While swimming, he heard a woman's voice coming somewhere around a group of trees beside the stream. It was a voice that was different from any he'd ever heard. It was angelic in nature. He noticed a low puffy cloud near the trees, and there before his eyes was a beautiful woman urging him to walk to a spiritual church that was in a tiny village not too far from where he was. She told Joao there were people waiting for him. He was puzzled about this request, but he dried off and curiously went to this church. He entered the building, and that was all he remembered until he woke up hours later. An elder told him that he instantaneously healed many people in those few hours and performed amazing surgeries. Joao felt that the elderly man wasn't telling the truth, but he began conversing as he ate his meal while sitting with those he healed. One by one they came forward with their illness stories, and then they seemed to be cured. He was then convinced. The woman with the angelic voice was St. Rita of Cassia."

"We don't hear too much about St. Rita. I've only heard stories like that in movies or books!" June replied, noticeably rattled.

"But why is he called *John of God?*" she asked.

My mother sat there in silence, waiting.

"St. John of God helped the poor and distressed. And Joao has helped thousands with healing and cures, and also has fed and clothed the local, disadvantaged people in his community for over forty years."

"Very thought-provoking," commented June as she considered the information.

"Yes, pretty outlandish! I wouldn't be convinced unless I had first-hand experience and—my, oh my—I saw some unusual things," I replied.

"Okay, let me explain the entity part," I continued.

"Apparently, Joao incorporates spirits who were here on earth at one point and some who were not. I've been told many can come through, but only a certain few are with him all the time, like St. Ignatius of Loyola. And a physician, Dr. Augusto, who I felt was present while I was at The Casa. Also, other beings like St. Francis Assisi and King Solomon. I learned that he cannot incorporate some, like the spirit of King Solomon, given that Joao begins to bleed out his nose and ears.

It's too much for his body to endure. I didn't see this, but others have. One day, when I went up to John of God to get instructions, I felt a need to put my hand over his. It was stiff—hard, like he wasn't there. It felt like he was dead. When Daddy died and I was at his casket the night before his service, I placed my hand on his and it felt just like that. I was told that the spirits take over his body to heal others. It's called *incorporating*."

"Wow, that's unreal!" June was not sure about the entity part.

"I don't believe it!" My mother butted in.

"You got to be there to believe it, Mom," I replied.

"There are people who don't accept it, like you, but they haven't been there, or even if they have been to The Casa, they didn't stay the two weeks recommended. One must stay at least two weeks. First, it's vital to adapt to the incredible energy there. The place is built on a vortex, which is an area where electromagnetic collective energy has been said to move in a swirling motion. It has a vast crystal rock bed underneath. Crystals play a huge role in healing. Most people discount this ancient knowledge, but if they took interest to research and travel to the places known for these phenomena, their opinions might change. This was why Abadiania was chosen for the healing center. Second, one needs to settle into the life of meditation and healing mode. One must meditate twice a day, three days a week at the center. And it's not unusual to meditate three to five hours per session. Five hours is a very long stretch to meditate for most not accustomed to this lifestyle," I continued.

"It was mentioned that groups of people meditating could bring up the energy level. Apparently, energy plays a huge role in healing others. And it appears to be a natural anesthesia and guards against infection. I remember witnessing John of God doing eye surgery in the main hall of The Casa. He was standing before a full house when he took a kitchen knife and scraped a blind man's eyes. I had to turn away as it was beyond anything I've ever heard or seen. It almost made me ill. The eyes are so sensitive, but imagine such a thing with no anesthesia! And the man had no infection after."

"I can't even imagine. I'm getting queasy just imagining it. No infection, ever?" June shivered in her seat, staring into the rear view mirror.

"That is what I heard," I told them.

"I also had a chance to talk with a nursery school teacher from Canada, who was my neighbor at the posada where I was staying. She had this same procedure as well because she was tired of wearing glasses. I was told it hurt but not as much as we may expect. She had to rest for a few days, with her eyes closed. In fact, everyone was instructed after a surgery that they must rest twenty-four hours. There were people who didn't obey this advice and went sightseeing instead, only to have their health issue intensified. Most people do not feel that they've even had a surgery. Often it's non-invasive on the surface, which is totally perplexing. But I did chat with a few who were miserable when they didn't obey the instructions. One man from Santa Cruz had a degenerative eye problem. He had a surgical operation and didn't rest. His issue worsened and he ended up returning to Abadiania for two more visits."

"This is sounding like a Rod Sterling segment on TV." June was now convinced this was all sci-fi material.

"Yes, it almost appears that way," I laughed.

I paused, hesitating to continue.

"John of God can heal through photos. I brought Michael's photo. His brain surgery is coming up in about a week, and I thought this could help."

"Yes, we plan to visit," June tenderly replied, and my mother nodded with concern.

I continued to stare at June's face through the driver's mirror. She was distracted and having some trouble concentrating on her driving while we were in stop-and-go traffic. A second later, we were at a dead stop in our lane. June wanted to move into another lane since she wanted to exit the freeway, but no one would let her. Someone laid on his screeching horn! We all turned our heads in a disturbed manner, since we had been preoccupied. We finally broke free, but a small sports car pulled right in front of our van and almost cut us off! We braced ourselves and took deep breaths to relax.

"Jesus, Mary, and Joseph!" my mother exclaimed as she jumped. My sister shook her head, and I just tuned out, daydreaming of the beginning of my journey to Abadiania, Brazil.

3: One Soul's Journey

San Francisco Airport—Early December 2001 (Three Months after

9/11)

I sat and waited for my name to be called from the standby list. I was on pins and needles. Different names were announced but not mine.

If I don't get on this flight, there is no other flight to Miami today. I pondered the thought, and it made me uneasy. I would have to call my son, Jonathan, to come back and get me. He would have to drive once again to San Francisco the next day, and I would have to repeat the standby ritual.

Jonathan was probably almost home by now, and I was sure he wouldn't be too thrilled if I summoned him. I prayed to my angel Gertie, an angel who always assists when I ask, and pleaded for a seat. Those who were standing around the general area were now on the aircraft. There were a few people sitting, reading, and not paying much attention. Finally, one last name was called.

"Cynthia Long, please come to the podium."

I jumped up, thanking God, Gertie and my angel team for the last seat on the plane. This journey was meant to be!

As I eagerly check out the seat assignment on my ticket while walking toward the aircraft, I gasped. It was way to the back of the plane. As I slowly moved toward the rear of the aircraft, the entire flight was filled to capacity.

But at this point, I was grateful and more than ready to move on to my next adventure.

I had to literally climb over two passengers to get to my seat. They didn't budge an inch to make this an easy task. I was squashed like a sardine. I held my bathroom duty until my bladder was screaming at me. Resting was almost impossible. Reading was the second challenge. The reading light wasn't working properly; it hit one of my neighbors straight in the eyeballs. I remembered my manners and gave up the idea of using the light. I hoped they appreciated the gesture, though I didn't think they even noticed. I couldn't wait for the flight to end!

Finally, at 11:30 p.m., we landed in Miami, Florida. I had to rush to catch the next leg of my flight since it was the only one to Brazil. I found a place to stand near the gate area, and I watched the passengers board the flight. I began counting those left.

"Wow, there are so many standbys," I babbled out loud.

An uneasy feeling came over me like a giant wave. *If I don't make this flight, what will plan "B" be?* At that point, I had never been stranded anywhere before while flying standby.

As a woman traveling alone, this situation was alien, and I wasn't excited to have to sort this out all by myself at such a late hour. Three names were called, and none was mine.

There was a gentleman standing near me who was talking out loud to himself in a Brazilian accent. We peered at each other in uncertainty.

"I cannot believe I didn't get on this flight. I don't know what to do. This has never happened." I was clearly shaken and blurted out each word in disbelief. I leaned hard against the wall, as if it was the wall's fault my name was not called.

"I can't believe it either," the Brazilian man responded. We began walking with the other handful of standbys.

"Where do we stay?" I continued. "It's almost 1:00 a.m. We cannot stay here!" I was still disturbed and caught up in the fear.

"I'm so sorry. I'm Cynthia," I finally laughed as I realized I'd forgotten my manners. The man distressingly looked at me as if he was just as upset about our problem.

"Hello, I'm Marco. Nice to meet you. Let's go to the airline desk and ask."

We rushed down the ramp pulling our carry-ons behind us.

"If worse comes to worse, we can look for a room at a hotel my company is associated with and perhaps get a discount."

I'm glad my angel Gertie guided me to stand next to Marco. *What a blessing!* I thought to myself.

We checked with the airline desk, and they gave us a discount voucher for a hotel, but it wasn't a very good deal. Marco and I stepped away. Marco pulled out his phone, called for assistance, and located a hotel. The rate was half off. We walked quickly outside. He immediately flagged a taxi, took my bags, and assisted the taxi driver as they loaded them into the car.

The hotel was very comfortable, but we didn't have the luxury to enjoy it much since we were preoccupied. We went back and forth to the airport every day for three days, with no luck of getting out of Miami. The airport was full of travelers that early-December—the first big flying month after 9/11. Each day there was disappointing news: no seats on any of the various flights to San Paulo, where Marco lived and I was booked for the next leg of the trip.

What was so fascinating was that Marco and I turned into fast friends. This doesn't happen often. We divulged quite a bit about our lives during those three days. Each morning he would wait downstairs in the lobby to join him for breakfast. It was like we'd been friends forever. As soon as I mentioned my spiritual connection, he thought it was odd for an American to have such knowledge and information. I was curious why he thought that, but later found out that he had been a foreign exchange student living near Los Angeles at one point and noticed that no one he met was into anything spiritual in those days. What he didn't realize was that things were changing now in the US. People were waking up!

I mentioned to Marco earlier on that I was heading to Abadiania, a small community two hours from Brasilia to see the faith healer, John of God. He got very agitated. Marco revealed alarming stories of people who had gone on these types of adventures and were never seen again. That sort of bothered me. I asked if he knew John of God. He had never heard of him. He thought that was even more of a concern. Marco mentioned that his cousin lived close to Brasilia and would call and ask about this so called "healer."

"Cintia, there are crazy people in Brazil. I'm worried about you! Please be careful," Marco responded with uncertain big eyes.

This topic was brought up each day. And it was almost as though Marco wanted to talk me out of going. I mentioned that I had done a lot of research before I had made a decision to go on this journey. I'd also arranged to meet a guide and a friend who were already in Abadiania. And before I committed to the trip, I had references of those who had just returned. Each had their own phenomenal story! I was encouraged to go. These individuals were working mainstream jobs and had a spiritual base to their life. I only had half an ear on what Marco was saying, but he patiently listened to what I had to say. Still, I wondered what he thought of me.

4: Travels with Marco and the Wild Brazilian Taxi Ride

Those three days were long and tiring, but Marco made it easier by sharing some of his life story.

He talked to his wife, Maria, off and on while we waited for our flights. She worked for an airline in Brazil and suggested a clever idea to help get us on our way.

"Maria mentioned maybe we should fly to Rio, where my mother lives, and stay there one night. She could take us to the airport the next day. What do you think, Cintia?"

I pondered his wife's suggestion. "Marco, your mother doesn't even know me. You are inviting a total stranger to her home?" I was walking and talking, almost by myself, as Marco was already at the second podium asking about the flight loads.

After talking to the attendant with Brazilian passion, Marco replied, "Cintia, in Brazil we do such things. You worry too much!"

Really? After repeating his statement in my mind, I thought about how most people are not that overly generous. And the majority would feel I was not wise to stay in a stranger's home.

Finally through the third ticket agent, we were booked to fly to Rio. We got the last available seats, and we were ecstatic! We rushed to the gate. All the passengers were loaded, and we literally waited only a minute for our names to be called.

The airport was beyond crazy! I had never seen so many security people. The lines to the gates were no doubt unreal. Again, this was back in the early days after 9/11. It was the first time travelers were expected to take off their shoes. We finally got through the incredible maze of endless lines and headed for the gate. That terrible day changed the course of all our lives in more ways than one. Our seats were first class accommodations. As we buckled up, we were giggling like children on a magic carpet ride! I thanked God and my angels again for this breakthrough.

Throughout the flight, Marco continued to insist that I stay at his mother's home.

"Cintia, you are going to stay with me and my mother."

I just didn't know what to say except that his mother needed to know way before we showed up. "Marco, after you speak to your mother, I'll feel more comfortable," I replied affectionately.

* * *

As we landed, my stomach was full of butterflies. I had a feeling this trip would be one of the wildest of my life.

The San Paulo airport was virtually empty as we arrived after midnight. Marco pulled out his phone immediately, pushed a few buttons, waited, spoke a little Portuguese, and flipped his phone shut.

"It's settled! We will take a cab to my mother's home and will make arrangements for our flight to San Paulo in the morning."

We drove through Rio. I was sort of perplexed. Rio had always been advertised as a very romantic and happening place, adorned with inviting beaches. To be fair, maybe I needed spend more time to capture what's been written and touted.

We got to our destination. There was a grouping of condominium-style homes. We climbed a series of cement stairs, got into a small elevator and then entered a building to his mother's home.

Fatima, sixty-something, a gracious Brazilian woman, greeted us at the door. I was welcomed and ushered around Fatima's humble home and then guided to the modest room where I would sleep. Fatima kindly asked Marco in Portuguese if I was thirsty or hungry, which I wasn't. I settled in and walked into the living area, where Marco and his mother were talking a mile a minute. It was like they hadn't seen each other in a blue moon and were best friends. It was comforting to witness this bond of a mother and son.

Fatima inquired about my life in the US. Marco translated our conversation, which took awhile seeing that she had many curious questions. The subject of spirituality and paranormal entities was brought up. Marco's mother had different experiences throughout her life, so I was now the one asking the questions. She mentioned a local spiritualist church where paranormal occurrences happened at a constant rate. I could not talk to most people in the States about phenomena like this because they would assume I was off my rocker! I'd had such experiences, but was a little fearful to share them until now. I hesitated, changed the subject, and mentioned to Fatima that my grandfather's roots were in Brazil. I felt like I was finally home. That statement was such a comforting feeling, which allowed me to relax. A quick glance at the clock showed it was three in the morning. I stood and expressed my goodnight and thank-you's. Marco and Fatima chatted away until who knows when.

It was hot and muggy in Rio. I tossed and turned all night long. A swamp cooler in the small bedroom window was turned to the maximum capacity, but still I had no relief.

The next morning I awoke to Marco and his mother chatting away in the kitchen. I had little breakfast since nothing offered sounded appetizing. Perhaps it was the sleepless night or the excitement of what was in store in Abadiania that affected my appetite. We talked about the plan for the day. After our showers, we packed our things and drove toward the coastal route.

I definitely played the tourist part. My head turned completely around more than once. One of the things that was surprising, women wore very revealing clothing. It was as if no one even noticed. Men didn't gawk, even the homeless men on the streets. I asked Marco about it.

"In Brazil, we are not modest and don't hide our bodies like those in the States. This is accepted here." Marco turned toward me and was very serious about this statement.

Fatima pressed on as Marco asked her to drive to the famous statue of *Christ the Redeemer*. The iconic figure was located atop Corcovada Mountain. As we drove up the mountain, I got chills viewing this massive and beloved statue of Jesus. I snapped photos of the enormous sculpture, and to this day, it's one of my favorite photographs. This was a part of Rio that was clearly impressive.

After taking the photos, we disembarked the mountain driving toward the airport to catch our flight. I wished I had more time to spend with Fatima. I would have loved to get to know her better and experience the spiritualist church she talked of so fondly. Someday I will do so, after this book is completed and I have one to hand her!

Fatima pulled up to the airport departure area, and we all got out. I felt a pang of sadness when we said our goodbyes. But I knew there was an adventure ahead. I gave Marco's mother a big hug and thanked her for her hospitality.

"We will meet again soon," she said in Portuguese.

Marco and I walked away, aiming toward the airline podium to get my ticket. He insisted on seeing me to the gate as well. *What a gentleman!*

"Here is my phone number, Cintia. Please call and keep me posted on this wild adventure of yours! I'm still not convinced that this community is on the up-and-up!"

"I will." I took the scrap of paper with his number and held it tightly.

"Promise?"

"I promise." I hugged Marco and watched him disappear into the crowd.

The flight was about an hour long. I nervously questioned whether there would be anyone to pick me up at the airport since my arrangements were all verbal communication over the phone and by e-mail thousands of miles away. Each reference warned that this was a third-world country and to be patient, especially since I did not speak their language. I thought to myself, *Got to let Gertie and the angel team handle this and guide me.*

Arriving without delay, I gathered my luggage and entered an area where there were lots of people waiting and moving about. Scouting the area, there among the crowd was a middle-aged man holding a brown cardboard sign, torn from a box, with the word *Cintia* on it.

I picked up my pace and almost hugged him while approaching. He spoke no English. I placed my hand to my chest and said, *"Cynthia!"*

He smiled and pointed to the street outside. I gulped back my apprehension and followed him to his taxi.

Welcome to Brazil, I said to myself while I trailed behind. *Let the excitement begin!*

The ride to Abadiania took a few hours. I perused my handbag for the Portuguese translation book I had packed, just in case. It proved to be useless when I made attempts to ask questions. The driver had no clue of what I was saying. I then began pointing to each word. That didn't work either. I wanted to throw it out of the window, but then something happened...

Out of nowhere, a large, old, rusty truck careened in front of us. I braced myself and screamed while focused on the back of the truck, which had the name *Apollo* and the number *23*. These two symbols had been very significant in my life. The driver panicked and scowled at me as if he didn't know what to do. I anxiously grabbed the translation book for one last desperate attempt to explain the significance. I anxiously pointed to more words and tried to pronounce them. I was beginning to conclude that he thought I was a crazy American!

I gave up and enjoyed the unbelievable synchronicity all by myself. I took a photo of the back of the truck. I knew some people would not believe it when I revealed such an amazing experience. I was in total disarray and kept saying out loud, "What are the odds of seeing the number 23 and Apollo together in a third-world country? And what are the odds that I would see the two symbols that have been so significant in my life?" If we were even a few minutes earlier or later, we would not have had this experience.

The driver appeared bewildered. I patted him on the shoulder to help ease his concern. This was for me and only me!

It took awhile to settle back down after such an incredible occurrence. I took deep breaths to calm myself. I scouted ahead and was mesmerized by the low odd-looking puffy clouds, which were just about hypnotic in nature. It was almost like visiting a different planet. I pointed at the billowing clouds and smiled at the taxi driver, giving him a small reason to forgive me for the outburst. He smiled back. I knew then that everything was okay.

It was very quiet after that. I began to daydream about the amazing synchronicity of 23 and Apollo.

5: Twenty-Three: In Route to another Dimension

Central Valley, California—1995

My youngest son, Jonathan, aged seventeen, and I were driving to meet my daughter, Allisa. We were going to attend the funeral of her then boyfriend's grandmother.

Jonathan mentioned while we were in route, that ever since he experimented with LSD, he began seeing the number 23. Jonathan sounded like he was haunted by it. He told of bizarre incidents of what he was experiencing.

"I look at the clock day after day only to see 4:23, 5:23, 6:23, and on, Mom. I went to get a meal at a fast-food restaurant, and the bill was $5.23. Just yesterday I got my new license plate, and it has the number 23 in it. It never ends!"

It sounded like Jonathan was seeing this number everywhere. He asked what I thought it meant. I had no clue to the answer. I thought it was a rather curious mystery, but I didn't want to put any more fuel to his uneasiness.

"Jon, it could be just a coincidence. I wouldn't worry about it."

Jonathan was mentally struggling back then anyway. Different things and situations bothered him, so I could see that this would end up eating at him more. Right after that conversation, we arrived at the address where we were to meet Allisa. Jonathan shakenly exclaimed, "Mom, look at the address!" Yes, it indeed had 23 in it. Feeling this was odd, I stopped and took a mental note.

Hana and Maui, Hawaii—1996

Jonathan and I went on a vacation to Maui shortly after that 23 sighting. Maui was the birthplace of my grandmother on my father's side. It's another very sacred and special place to visit. One day we wanted to drive to Hana. It's been stated that Hana is the last underdeveloped tropical paradise on Maui. A few people mentioned the wondrous hiking trails and beautiful waterfalls. Hana is a given, if people visit Maui. We noticed T-shirts everywhere with the inscription, "I survived Hana!" Jonathan and I questioned what that meant and wanted to check it out. It was a last-minute decision and, unfortunately, we got a late start. I didn't realize it would take as long as it did.

The roads were very narrow and harrowing—even one lane, at times, we had to make room for other cars. I now understood the *survived* part on the T-shirt. Once we arrived, shook up a little but in one piece, we briefly looked around, but not enough to explore the depth of Hana. I was a bit fidgety to get down the mountain and leery about the one-lane winding road, especially at night. It was pitch dark everywhere in Maui unless there was a full moon. I searched awhile for a place to turn around to get back to the main road and noticed an inviting driveway. I pulled in, and there before my eyes was the address: 23. Just 23. No other number! Jonathan shook his head with disbelief.

"Mom, look!" Jonathan pointed to the address I had already noticed. The jolt took my breath away, but I held my composure; Jonathan was very disturbed by this sighting.

I began seeing 23 on a daily basis after that, and periodically multiple times in a day. It was simply an amazing phenomenon! My friends and children know of the experiences I've had throughout the years. And now, some of my closest friends are seeing this number as well. As I write this now, two receipts from a store today had 23 in them. I called the phone company shortly after, because there was an error on my mother's cell phone bill that I needed to straighten out. When the agent deducted the two charges, the total came out to $23.23. These are just a few of the thousands of experiences with the number 23.

6: Apollo, Abadiania, and Mystery of the Internet

Sunnyvale, California—1997, After the Maui Vacation with Jonathan

I had to purchase a particular beer for a guest coming to dinner and asked the clerk where the brand was located. I was directed to the coolers and I almost bumped into a beer named Apollo. Apollo beer? Never heard of it!

When I returned from the store, I was putting the groceries away and noticed for the first time the name Apollo on the water heater in the pantry.

Okay, this was twice now in one day. I asked myself if Apollo would be the next symbol coming into my life.

A few weeks went by and I had an interview with a potential client. I was sitting on this man's sofa, looking for a way to start up a conversation. A cat walked across the room. I asked what his name was.

He answered, "Apollo."

"What?" I said in disbelief.

A few weeks later, I needed to go to the book store. I was walking down one of the aisles when a book fell off the shelf. I curiously glanced over my shoulder and turned to pick it up. It had the title *Apollo Space Shuttle*. I thumbed through to see if there would be anything in it to give a clue or message. Nothing. I never hit any of the books or shelves as I walked past them. I put it back on the shelf, in awe, and carried on. I found the book I was looking for, purchased it, and then, in route to my then-boyfriend's home, I made a wrong turn. I was lost, which wasn't unusual. A bit frustrated, looking for familiar streets, I stumbled onto the street Apollo. *Seriously!*

A week or so went by, I was sitting in the living room TV surfing. I landed an interview with a young man who was in the Olympics—Apollo. Who in this day and age has the name Apollo?

Apollo comes in and out of my life, but 23 is a constant.

* * *

This brings me back to the taxi ride. The driver and I made the journey to the small village of Abadiania. Glancing out of the car window, I noticed a dusty and somewhat backward community with horses and cows sharing the road. The driver removed my luggage, and I followed the uneven stone pathway to the makeshift office to check in. The owner of the posada was a blonde-haired, blued-eyed, middle-aged woman. She did not look Brazilian in my book. I didn't know back then that there was a German influence in Brazil. She graciously helped me to my room.

As we entered, I was amused by the sight: two hard looking twin beds, an old semi painted shelf, and a light that dangled from the ceiling by a wire. I then entered the bath area. There was a sink and toilet with a showerhead in the same proximity of the toilet. The owner proceeded to mention that no toilet paper could be flushed down the toilet since their system was fragile.

Bewildered by this news and wondered where the private matter ended up.

"Toilet paper is placed in a bag and put outside in front each day for someone to dispose of." I'd never heard of this before and was a bit grossed out, but then shook off my disturbance. The posada owner moved on as if it was no big deal and mentioned that John of God would be at The Casa on Wednesday, Thursday, and Friday. It was already Tuesday evening.

"Go look around," she replied in a thick Brazilian accent. I asked for directions and the whereabouts of my guide. I was told she was in the dining room since it was dinnertime.

* * *

I snapped back to the present when my sister hit the driveway curb at our mother's home where I was temporarily living. We all got out and my sister helped with my luggage. I was now feeling a bit worn out and ready to take a nap. But I couldn't resist checking my e-mail. I'd only had minimal computer access during my month-long visit in Abadiania.

I placed my luggage in my bedroom and scooted over to the computer room. My mother followed. She wanted to converse more since I had been away for awhile and appeared to have missed me. I took a seat at my computer desk. I logged in and was welcomed by eight e-mails from a paid dating site, which I hadn't been a member of in a few years.

"That's odd," I murmured.

"What's that?" My mother asked.

I didn't reply. I was too preoccupied.

I clicked on each e-mail. One was a very familiar face. I stared intently. It was a guy I had met back in the '70s at a college party.

"Wow, I met this guy in the '70s at a party."

"For real?" my mother asked.

I was consumed in the moment. I skimmed the e-mail and moved on to the others.

"Are you going to respond?" My mother was curious.

"I don't think so." I closed the e-mail, stood up from my computer chair, and got into the shower. I began reminiscing.

7: Friendship or a Love Connection?

San Jose, California—May 1970

The modest house was filled with college students. There were little groupings here and there, chatting away. Five guys stood near the kitchen sink, surrounding one guy. They were betting that he wouldn't dare take bites out of a wine glass and swallow the pieces. The guy, Randy, a very well-known baseball star, was the crazy one! He was wearing a pocket T-shirt, jeans, and athletic shoes. Wild. I remember it vividly now.

Why has this unimportant detail come to me? I couldn't remember what I wore back then, let alone someone I'd just met and who wasn't even a love interest. It was 1970, the days of the Vietnam War. Those graduating from college with a low draft number meant bound for Vietnam. This was the end of the beatnik era and a lead into the hippy movement, which made the phrase *flower power* popular, widely used in conversation, and accepted throughout the nation—and probably the world. Flower power meant passive resistance to peacefully transform protests that flared up during the Vietnam conflict. Love, not war, was celebrated, revered, and went hand-in-hand with the iconic peace sign that hippies flashed wherever they went; it is still practiced by young and old worldwide today. Rock and roll was an important part of the baby boomers' culture. It gave them a support system, which freed them from the grip of parental control and society's rules and regulations geared to force them into a cookie-cutter existence.

We were the first generation who had the courage to question authority in a big way in comparison to the generations before us. It has been said that we were the largest generation ever, and that we were the ones who broke the mold for the following generations. Most of our parents misunderstood this radical movement. I was too fearful of joining the movement due to my father's stronghold. My father and I had a few differences of opinion and disagreements, but I was never interested in pushing too far. I observed the events that unfolded during that era, which were totally mind blowing. *The Love In's*, psychedelic-anything, and some other odd behaviors of those going to the extreme were alarming to witness. I knew teens that blew their minds on LSD. Sadly, a few to this day are still struggling.

Those who followed musicians were also following what was happening in different areas of the country. Greenwich Village was a world away from California, but I would hear or read about some of the events there. Photographs of musicians embracing bare-studded guitars strapped to their backsides, many unknown musicians ended up roaming the streets in Greenwich Village, gathering at hot spots in hope they would be discovered. The likes of Arlow Guthfry and Peter, Paul, and Mary were still popular, but the shift began when the Beatles arrived on American soil. Parents were extremely bothered that they were a worldwide sensation. The effects they had on most every family with teenagers were evident. The Beatles were my favorite group. They were not welcomed by my parents due to their long hairstyle. Yet they were dressed in suits and properly mannered.

The Stones, Jefferson Airplane, Grateful Dead, and Bob Dylan pushed the musical limits. Crosby, Stills, Nash & Young were earthy guys. Other favorites were the Beach Boys who were the surfer types, which matched their music genre. I adored James Taylor and still do, like millions around the world. His music is timeless. I enjoyed Judy Collins and Carol King; they rode the wave of the shifting tide. It's been stated that songs in this era changed many people and virtually world views, especially among the baby-boomer generation.

Could the drug and sexual revolution be the driving force that contributed to the changes? If one takes those two components away, would there have been such a huge shift in consciousness? For example, we witnessed the Beatles making that wide leap, which in turn, led their followers down that path. From the day they appeared in the US, their symbolic hairstyle was a main topic in most people's conversations. They certainly set the stage for hairstyles among young men, which led to other changes. What's so amusing is that if we now glance at the Beatles past photos, the opinion of what was considered scary to our parents wasn't anything compared to what was to unfold when other groups arrived. Later in the Beatles' career, they began soul searching, which led them to India. This began a new phase in their life and in others, and in turn their music changed its course.

Most young women wore wide-legged, bell-bottom jeans, min-iskirts, and knee boots. Long and straight-ironed hair was very popular. Jocks and semi-hippy-looking young men were abundant in my life. My father condemned those who grew their hair like the rock stars pic-tured on vinyl records that were collected and displayed in teenage rooms. If only one lock of hair reached their shirt collar, they were not allowed in our home. Smoking was popular—cigarettes and pot.

Coming back to the moment, I recollected how all the guys had put their bets on the kitchen counter, voices raised in excitement. Randy carefully bit on the wine glass. Chewing slowly and then cautiously swallowing the pieces. Everyone roared, cheered, oohed, and aahed! I thought he was absolutely nuts as I stared in disbelief. I walked away toward a group of young women who were talking about this nutty guy.

* * *

I stepped out of the shower not wanting to accept that Randy's reemergence was a random occurrence. I thought out loud, *Glass-eating Randy, and he's still alive? And he e-mails me from a dating site I hadn't been a member of in two years and doesn't even recognize me? Very strange!*

A few weeks passed. My attention continued to point toward contacting Randy. *Maybe I should just write to that crazy guy Randy to let him know who I was.* I was a bit reluctant. I wasn't in a place to date anyone and didn't want to give him the wrong impression. But for some reason, I felt pushed to respond. Regularly I get nudges like that and question what it's about. I searched for the e-mail, found it, and wrote the following note:

To: randy@yahoo.com

From: cindy@gmail.com

Time: 10:00 p.m.

Subject: Hello

Hello Randy,

I'm Cindy. I was married to Lance A. Do you remember me?

When I opened your e-mail, I said to myself, I know this guy! I remember you were the one who took a few bites of a wine glass at a Stanford College party in the '70s. I thought, wow, he's still alive! Hahaha...

Cindy

An evening later I received his reply.

To: cindy@gmail.com

From: randy@yahoo.com

Time: 9:00 p.m.

Subject: Re: Hello

Cindy,

Of course I remember you! I didn't recognize you in the photos. How have you been all of these years?

Randy

And a day later, sent another message to him.

To: randy@yahoo.com

From: cindy@gmail.com

Time: 4:00 p.m.

Subject: Re: Hello

Randy,

I'm fine. Don't know if you heard, Lance and I got a divorce after twenty years of marriage.

I haven't been on this dating website in a few years. I was away for a month and came back to eight e-mails? I was sort of confused with it all.

Cindy

A day later.

To: cindy@gmail.com

From: randy@yahoo.com

Time: 5:00 p.m.

Subject: Re: Hello

Cindy,

I was actually looking for someone and went to a local search of Sunnyvale, and there you were!

Glad I found you!

Yes, I was sorry to hear about your divorce.

Would you like to have dinner sometime?

Randy

A day later.

To: randy@yahoo.com

From: cindy@gmail.com

Time: 7:21 p.m.

Subject: Re: Hello

Hi Randy,

Not interested in dating. Thanks anyway!

Cindy

Same day.

To: cindy@gmail.com

From: randy@yahoo.com

Time: 8:10 p.m.

Subject: Re: Hello

Cindy,

Let's catch up! No strings attached!

Randy

I struggled with his statement "no strings attached." I didn't have a social life and had just gotten back from an intense month-long retreat.

Maybe just a harmless dinner? I thought to myself.

Again, there was that nudge I didn't care to feel. I was not interested in dating Randy, plain and simple! *Where is all this coming from?*

I went about my daily life. Work, work, and more work!

Four days later.

To: cindy@gmail.com

From: randy@gmail.com

Time: 6:23 p.m.

Subject: Re: Hello

Hi Cindy,

Hope I didn't scare you away?

Randy

Same day.

> To: randy@yahoo.com
>
> From: cindy@gmail.com
>
> Time: 7:23 p.m.
>
> Subject: Re: Hello
>
> *Hi Randy,*
>
> *No, just don't want a relationship right now.*
>
> *Cindy*

Same day.

> To: cindy@gmail.com
>
> From: randy@yahoo.com
>
> Time: 10:32 p.m.
>
> Subject: Re: Hello
>
> *Cindy,*
>
> *Not to worry! No strings attached. I'd like to take you to Carmel and then to Monterey to a casual diner that's a favorite of mine. Are you busy next weekend?*
>
> *Randy*

Two days later. After tossing the idea around and also talking with a friend, I reluctantly accepted the offer.

> To: randy@yahoo.com
>
> From: cindy@gmail.com

Time: 5:23 p.m.

Subject: Re: Hello

Randy,

I'm free next Sat.

Cindy

Same day.

To: cindy@gmail.com

From: randy@yahoo.com

Time: 10:11 p.m.

Subject: Re: Hello

Hi Cindy,

Great! I can't wait to see you.

Randy

* * *

Los Gatos—Day of the Date

I was still feeling uneasy about this casual dinner and friends-only date, but I had a very strong feeling that it was vital to go for some reason I couldn't discern.

I waited in the car in the parking lot, looking for Randy. I noticed a man with short blonde hair, glasses, and some extra weight get out of his car. I followed suit and we both walked toward each other. He had changed dramatically since college. He was in great athletic shape back then. It appeared like he wasn't taking care of himself.

Randy walked up to hug me.

"Cindy, you look the same."

I thought a moment.

"Really?" I wasn't sure he was telling the truth.

"You look great." Randy politely, but nonchalantly eyed my body.

It was very kind of him to say so, but I couldn't return the compliment. I complimented his stylish glasses and left it at that. I changed the subject as I was preoccupied that my car would be towed since the posted signs were confusing. He assured me the car was fine.

We approached Randy's car, and he graciously opened the door. I took a mental note. Randy stopped by the ocean to view the beautiful coastal scenery as we drove toward Carmel. He wanted to get out and take a good look at the gorgeous view. I agreed. We stood by the car. Randy casually moved in a bit close. I backed away just a wee bit not to be rude. He noticed and honored that decision. I took another mental note.

We got to Carmel and spent a few hours walking up and down the quaint streets, window shopping. It was a beautiful day and Carmel was crowded. Randy found a great area to relax and people watch. He sat too close for comfort, so I moved just a tad. We finished our time in Carmel. We were now en route for Monterey.

There was some catching up to do after thirty years. Randy kept me laughing all the way to the restaurant.

8: The Strange Eye Contact in Monterey

We got to the dock in Monterey, and Randy parked the car near the restaurant.

"As I mentioned in my e-mail to you, this is a very casual eatery, but it's a favorite of mine." Randy again kindly opened the passenger side of the car and graciously helped me out. We walked to the steep steps that led straight down to the seaside restaurant. It was just as he said. It was a very modest place on the water. Couples scattered throughout. Randy searched around for a window seat, but they were all taken. An older waitress with her hair in a twist took us to a table, but Randy wasn't happy with the choice.

"Is there a table coming up by the window?"

The waitress scanned the area. "Not just yet. I can seat you here, and you can move when something comes available."

"Sounds good."

Randy and I had some small talk, then family talk. I excused myself to use the ladies room. Randy stood and slid my chair out from the table. As I left the table and walked away, I noticed Randy sat back down. When I returned, Randy rose from his seat and pulled out my chair once again. He had the manners of a West Point officer. No one except my late father displayed that sort of attribute in my life. I was impressed. I took more notes.

The dinner salad arrived, and a group of diners left one of the window seats. Randy called the waitress over, and she helped us move. We reminisced and laughed a lot. I tried not to use a lot of eye contact;

I didn't want to lead him on. I've had perplexing circumstances with other men throughout my life—when I stared into their eyes too often, they got the impression I was interested in them. Randy was charming and very nice, but I was not interested in him romantically. At the end of dinner, I had to use the ladies' room once more. Randy, with a smile on his face, stood again until I was about to enter the ladies' room. Upon returning, I walked toward the table, I caught Randy's eyes, and something clicked—a remembrance. *What is this?* I got a feeling I'd known him before. And not in the '70s—some other time. Was it a past life connection? This had never happened with any other man. Our eyes locked for a few seconds, and then I shifted my attention just beyond his right shoulder, a comfort zone of sorts for me. Randy assisted with my chair once again, and we continued our conversation. We unquestionably hit it off, like old friends, but I was disappointed in myself since I felt this short encounter of locking of eyes might bring an undesirable situation down the road.

All I wanted was to be friends with this man! Friends only! I repeated under my breath all the way home.

Our drive back to Los Gatos was faster than the way over to Monterey, so it felt. We were having an enjoyable afternoon reminiscing. Randy parked near my car, got out, opened the passenger door, and offered his hand to help me out of the car. We walked to my car, he asked for my keys, opened the door, and shut it once I was safely inside. I rolled the window down to chat for a few more minutes. We hugged through the open window and both left in our respective automobiles.

I was in deep thought about our day. I was pulled in so many different directions. I was a bit disappointed when I locked eyes with Randy, as I did not want a relationship. He acted hopeful looking back into my eyes. I was restless all night long. The next day I called my friend.

"Hi Jen..."

"Well, how did it go?" She knew I was going to call with the details.

I paused.

"It was fun but I only want to be friends. He tried a few instances to get close, but I moved. Something happened, though, at dinner, and I don't know what to make of it."

I began sharing the eye contact connection, but Jen did not want to hear anything about it.

"Just have fun. You don't have a social life right now, and if he's fun...go with the fun!"

"I guess so, but it was very unusual," I responded, half disturbed.

Jen almost interrupted, stopped herself and was plainly not interested.

"Just have fun! Forget the rest! You worry too much!"

We then changed the subject and completed our conversation.

The next morning I opened my e-mail and here's what I found.

To: cindy@gmail.com

From: randy@yahoo.com

Time: 11:30 p.m.

Subject: Thank you!

Hi Cindy,

Thanks for the wonderful time.

Randy

I took another mental note. I closed the message and proceeded to the next.

Two days later, Randy called. "Hi, Cindy. I'm going to be in Los Gatos for business on Friday. Do you want to meet for a drink?"

I paused. I sorted through my mind on the week ahead and then Friday. Nothing exciting happening.

"Okay."

Randy began a conversation about one of his friends. "You remember Jeff Mitchell?"

I was surprised he brought up Jeff! Jeff was a friend of my former husband and was in our wedding.

"Yes, how is he?" I was inquisitive since I hadn't heard anything about Jeff in a long while.

"He's good. He's living in the East Bay and has started his own company."

"Oh, really? What sort of company?" I asked, still curious for more information.

"He started a marketing company and is working with start-ups."

"Interesting. When did you become friends?" I was still not clear on how they knew each other.

"Let's see, it was maybe fifteen years ago? I ran into him playing golf, and we've been friends ever since."

"He and I went to a Warriors basketball game the other night, and I mentioned your name."

I didn't want to talk about it any further and changed the subject. Randy went on and on, but the curious part was that Jeff was now his friend. We both needed to run and agreed to catch up on Friday. We finished our conversation and hung up.

I said to myself, *Jeff and Randy are friends? That's wild!*

Thursday arrived and I got a call from Randy.

"Hi, lovely lady! Hope your day is going well!"

"Yes, so far, it's going okay," I casually replied.

"Good, mine has been insanely busy, and I'm about to rush off to church for a class. You should come with me on Sunday sometime."

"I haven't attended a Catholic church service in awhile," I replied. I paused, contemplating his offer. *What the heck?*

"Okay." I squeezed my eyes shut tight, not sure why I kept saying yes.

"Great!" Randy was overjoyed. "Talk to you soon, Cindy."

"Bye, Randy."

9: The Bizarre Signs

Friday I was in conversation with my mother, telling her about Randy. I mentioned the synchronicities that had occurred so far. She was strangely drawn to all the details about him.

I began preparing for our date, and realized I was running late and hurried along. I got in my car and noticed the clock, it was 6:23. I rushed to make the 6:30 date, but I was behind a slow-moving automobile. I wanted to pass, but traffic was backed up on each side. All of a sudden my eyes were fixated on the license plate in front of my car: 23. I almost screamed and shook my head in disbelief!

What is going on?

I hurriedly pulled into the restaurant and parked the car. I moved swiftly and entered through the elegant hand-carved, walnut double doors. My eyes landed on the ornate Italian vintage bar area, and there was Randy, waiting. He was spiffed up with a fresh haircut, fresh designer-framed eye glasses, cashmere blazer, and slacks. The host seated us and we ordered drinks. Randy began talking about his daughter, how close they were, and mentioned that he didn't want to date anyone until she finished college.

I took a note of this statement. I thought it to be very honorable that Randy's focus was on his daughter, and I was impressed with his commitment to her.

I mentioned the 23 incident that had just occurred as I was driving to the restaurant and a few other stories about 23. He was amused and wanted to know more. I felt pushed to bring to light this one particular story for some reason.

"I have a connection to this Catholic church in San Francisco, which the 23 mystery is a big part of."

Randy paused, as he contemplated.

"Why would you go to a church in San Francisco when you live in San Jose? There are many churches here." Randy was puzzled.

"There is a shrine dedicated to a saint there, and I have a deep connection to this saint. There are people from all over the globe who travel to this church to pray and ask for assistance. Countless miracles have occurred. I've also taken friends to the shrine—especially those facing adversities."

"Oh, I see...."

"The statue of Our Lady is very special too. It brought tears to my eyes when I encountered it. It feels like there's a shimmering light emitting from it."

Randy began to really tune into my story. He slowly sipped his drink and listened intently.

"One morning, a peculiar incident occurred. I woke up and for some reason zeroed in to a prayer card I had placed on the mirror in my bedroom. I felt almost pushed to take a closer look. I got up, pulled it off the mirror, and sat on the edge of bed to look at it. The address read '2390.' To even have the number 23 in it was wild! I then broke down the numbers and added them up (2+3+9+0=14 and 1+4=5), it added up to five (and so does 2+3), which I also thought to be weird since I see 23 everywhere!"

"What's the name of the church?" Randy asked.

I smirked and blurted out, "St. Joseph's." He was stone silent. He was undeniably frightened!

"What's wrong?" I was now concerned.

"My grandfather built that church!"

"No way!" I didn't believe him.

"Actually, he was the architect and was involved in the rebuilding after the earthquake in San Francisco."

I was speechless. I felt uncertain.

Randy was taken aback, now looking like there might be something more significant to these 23 stories. We changed the subject after we settled down. We finished up our drinks.

He walked me to my car and kissed me goodnight on the cheek.

"Thank you for the enjoyable evening, Cin. I'm intrigued by the 23 stories. Never quite met anyone like you before!"

I smiled and thought back to the comment he made about the church his grandfather built. I also wondered if there was something more going on here.

He asked for my keys, opened my car door, helped me in, and closed it.

"Goodnight, Randy. Thank you for the lovely evening."

"The pleasure is mine. Drive safe."

The car ride home was surreal. I kept going back to the fact that he said his grandfather rebuilt St. Joseph's Church. I was on the fence trying to wrap my head around believing Randy.

I got home and the phone rang. It was Randy.

"I just wanted to know you arrived safely."

"Yes, thank you. That's very sweet to call, Randy."

"Isn't this what every man should do after a date?" Randy replied.

"I believe so."

"We'll talk soon. Have a restful sleep."

"Thank you. Goodbye."

More note taking….

I called Jen the next morning.

"Hi, Jen. Do you have a minute?"

"Sure, what's up?"

I proceeded to reveal the church story and the connection with Randy's grandfather.

"Jen, what's your take?"

"Well, shoot, what are the odds of that? I don't know anyone who has built or even remodeled a church. Do you?"

"No one." I was baffled.

"This story is one for the books!" Jen spouted.

"I just don't know if I believe him."

"Why would he lie? And lie about something like that?"

"Don't know."

"Just wait and see. Time always reveals the truth," Jen added.

"Hey, Cin, how's Michael doing?" Jen asked.

"His brain surgery is in about a week." I responded.

"Let me know how the surgery goes?"

"Okay… Gotta run. Bye Jen."

"Okay… Bye."

* * *

Two days later, Randy called.

"Hey, Cindy. I have tickets to the Warriors basketball game in Oakland. Would you like to go on Friday night?"

I thought about Friday. Not much was going on, again. I hadn't been to a game in a long while.

"Okay."

"Great. Can you drive here? It's only about a half hour from my place."

"Sure."

We conversed a bit more and ended our conversation with laughter.

Friday afternoon arrived and I was driving up to San Ramon from San Jose. As I reached the freeway, I noticed a young man who was wearing a 23 jersey walking down the street.

Here we go again! I laughed to myself and wondered why 23 was a constant companion.

I got to Randy's place and called him when I was at the community gate. He was standing out by a beautiful waterfall waving and pointing to a parking area. He asked if I would like to see his home. I noticed a baby grand piano as I stepped inside.

"Do you play?"

"Not yet. It's on my bucket list."

Bucket list? I repeated to myself. I had never thought about a bucket list before. Maybe it would be a good idea to explore that plan!

We headed for Randy's car where he held the passenger door open. I found a gift between the two seats.

"I found this and thought of you." He was all smiles.

"That was sweet. Thank you!" I opened the small gift. It was a collectable item. I never collected those sorts of things, but it was a thoughtful gesture.

We talked all the way up to the game. I became preoccupied and quiet.

"Cin, what's wrong? You're quiet."

"Oh, I'm distracted and day dreaming about my son, Michael. He has major surgery coming up. He has a tumor on his pituitary gland. I feel he'll be alright, but it's a sensitive operation. There are many prayers going to the heavens for him right now."

"I'll place his name on St. Gregory's prayer list."

"Thank you." I fondly gazed at Randy.

Randy and I arrived, parked the car, and walked among the crowd of fans. Another guy wearing a 23 jersey cut in front of us. Our eyes met and we smiled. I mentioned the other kid that I had seen on the way to his place with a 23 jersey too. He laughed.

The basketball game was exciting. I found myself having a wonderful evening with Randy. We drove back to his place. He continued the gentlemanly courtesy and opened the car's passenger door. I was helped out and, again, he asked for my keys. We walked over to my vehicle and he opened my door. We hugged, he ushered me inside and shut the door. Randy seemed grateful for a wonderful evening. I drove home heartened and checked my e-mail before bed.

To: cindy@gmail.com

From: randy@yahoo.com

Time: 10:23 p.m.

Subject: Enjoyable evening

Cindy,

Again, it was a great evening. Thanks for your friendship.

Randy

I clicked reply.

To: randy@yahoo.com

From: cindy@gmail.com

Time: 10:32 p.m.

Subject: Re: Enjoyable evenings

Hi Randy,

It was a nice time. And thanks for the gift.

Cindy

I sent it off, closed my e-mail box, and went to bed. The next morning, I called my friend to discuss my feelings.

"Hi, Jen. Hey, I would like your opinion."

"I'm all ears!"

"I'm at a confused state. I'm in no position for a relationship, and Randy is not my type. He could be a wonderful friend, yes. Am I too shallow or what?"

My friend didn't care to go into the chemistry and discussion of feelings.

"Enjoy his company and friendship. He told you in the very beginning, no strings attached, didn't he? And you don't need chemistry for friendship! Cin, you have no social life! If he brings you joy, go for it!" Jen was direct and to the point, as usual.

"Yes, he did. But it doesn't feel like he's into just being friends. He's very nice, but friendship is all I want! I'm putting up walls on purpose, but I told him from the very start and he agreed!"

"Take down those walls, and just have fun!"

"Thanks, Jen."

"Anytime."

I checked my e-mail once more and Randy had sent a poem of friendship.

To: cindy@gmail.com

From: randy@yahoo.com

Time: 8:00 p.m.

Subject: Thank you

Hi Cindy,

I thought of you when I read this poem. Enjoy!

We met, it was luck

We talked, it was chance

We became friends, it was destiny

Thank you for your friendship, it is meant to be

Randy

I sat there restless. Was it luck and chance? Why did the uncomfortable feelings keep bubbling up?

* * *

The following week was a big one for my son, Michael. The day of the operation, I was by his side before he was wheeled into the surgery room. I placed a rosary around his neck. He had a crystal from Brazil and another rosary on his chest. He was in good spirits and joked around. Michael mentioned that his surgeon was very well known and had been on TV. I asked Michael about the program.

"He's been on the History Channel. He performed brain surgery on monkeys." Michael was proud of this.

"Brain surgery on monkeys?" I asked, not certain.

At that moment, Michael took notice of all the things on his chest. He acted a little embarrassed.

"Mom, thank you, but I think one rosary is enough." He was trying to be polite.

Michael carefully handed me the crystal and one rosary.

I took the rosary and crystal and put them in my pocket with another small rosary I'd brought. I had to use the ladies' room and needed to be very quick since I didn't want to miss when they were ready to wheel Michael into surgery. When I left the bathroom, I heard a woman sobbing behind a curtain just across the restroom. I stood there a minute wondering if I should intrude. It seemed like she had just received some bad news.

"Excuse me, ma'am? Can I come in?" I asked.

A quivering yes was the only response.

I opened the curtain just enough to peek in, not to impose too much.

"I heard you crying and thought to give you a gift I brought back from Brazil recently while I was on a spiritual journey. Do you believe in God?"

"Yes," she said as she sat there wiping her tears.

I took the extra rosary from my pocket and handed it to her.

"You must believe in miracles!" This burst out of my mouth, before I even realized.

Somehow, I guess I felt it was necessary for her to hear that.

She held the rosary in both hands, close to the middle of her chest, and responded, "yes."

"My son is just about to go into surgery. I must go but will pray for you. Take care," I said in a rushed voice.

"Thank you, so very much."

She spoke as if she thought this was almost an unreal situation occurring. I have always trusted that we are in the right place at the right time for a reason.

I hurried back. The thought of missing my son during a crucial moment was frightening. I approached Michael and my mother as they were conversing. Almost immediately two attendants arrived to whisk him away. I kissed his forehead and told him he would be fine. Michael eyed me and nervously smiled as he clutched the metal cross of the rosary in his hand.

My mother and I walked to the lobby and quietly waited.

I sat there and started meditating with my rosary and Brazilian crystal on my lap. After half an hour, I started praying. I asked for God's help, for the angels and John of God to assist in some way. Then, a mystifying incident happened.

Right before me, while my eyes were closed, I heard in Portuguese, "All is well. All is well!" I observed John of God's face in my mind's eye, and then poof...he vanished.

Hours went by. The doctor finally emerged to let us know that Michael did well and he was in recovery. As he was finally wheeled into his room, our family followed behind.

Michael was noticeably beat up; the surgical procedure was performed through the nose. He was coherent but drowsy.

"Michael, I'll be back tomorrow. Do you want anything special from the grocery store?" I waited attentively for his reply.

Michael shook his head no.

My mother and I kissed his forehead and said our goodbyes.

As we drove home, I told my mother of my experience in the waiting room.

"Mom, the strangest thing happened. I was praying, and I asked God, my angels, Michael's angels, and John of God to assist and to be present for Michael's surgery. I began meditating and all of a sudden, John of God's face flashed in my mind's eye. 'All is well. All is well.'

It was like a reassurance, but the funny thing is, he doesn't speak English. It was in Portuguese and I understood!"

My mother sat there with her mouth wide open. She gave the impression that I was freaking her out. "Cin, I saw him! I saw him!" My mother was traumatized.

"Saw who?"

"I saw John of God! He was walking toward the surgery room. I thought to myself, am I seeing this right? It can't be. Maybe it's someone who looks like him. The photo you showed me last week was the same man I saw walking into the operating room!"

"Are you serious? How is that possible?"

"I'm telling you what I saw. What I questioned was that he was wearing ordinary street clothes. I thought it was odd. But seconds later he was wearing hospital scrubs. How could that be? He made a change instantly"

"Now *I'm* feeling this is a *Twilight Zone* episode."

We drove home in silence. This was the most bizarre incident yet, and I did not know what to make of it.

The next day, I called a few friends and recounted this mystical story. They were all as spellbound as I was. No one I knew had ever heard anything remotely close to the story I told. I e-mailed a few new spiritual friends I'd met in Brazil, and each was perplexed and thought it was the coolest thing they'd ever heard!

I didn't feel comfortable telling Randy just yet since this was almost off the mainstream charts. Two months of seeing Randy came and went. Michael recovered, the tumor was benign. Life was good.

* * *

Randy and I went to a quaint Italian restaurant one evening. Over conversation, he asked if I wanted to spend the night since it was getting late and I was unusually tired.

"Cin, do you want to spend the night?"

"No, I need to drive home," I said.

"You can sleep in my bed, and I'll sleep in the other room?"

"No, I'm going home. Thank you, anyway."

* * *

Four Months Later

We were on our way to San Francicso for dinner one Saturday.

"Cin, do you mind if I drop off some papers at my mother's? Do you feel comfortable meeting her?"

"Sure, I'd like to meet your mother," I responded.

We drove up to her apartment and parked. Randy got out and performed his usual ritual of opening my car door, helping me out, and closing the door. We walked over to the apartment keypad that was situated in front of the building. Randy called his mother and she buzzed us in. We went up the elevator to her floor. Mrs. Walsh was down the hall waiting for us just outside her apartment front door.

"Hi, Mom, this is Cindy."

"Very nice to meet you, dear. I've heard a lot about you."

"Likewise." I made an effort to shake Mrs. Walsh's eighty-eight-year-old hand.

We went into the living area, and I sat on a small but inviting couch. Randy seated himself in a chair beside me. Mrs. Walsh was facing us next to the fireplace. I noticed above the fireplace was a portrait of her late husband, Randy's father. He was killed by a drunk driver while driving to work when Randy was only thirteen. Mrs. Walsh was pregnant with her eighth child then. She raised them all on her own. This tough-life situation was one I knew was filled with wisdom and lessons. I wanted to learn and grow from knowing Mrs. Walsh.

"So what's new, Mom?" Randy asked.

"Oh, not much."

I listened to her prattle on about "Aunt Lil this, Amanda that, grandchild this...."

I glanced around at the orderly home, not saying much.

"Mom, do you still have the brochure of St. Joseph's, the church that Grandfather rebuilt after the earthquake? That church is a favorite of Cindy's, and I thought she would like to have a copy."

"Oh, yes, I have a few left. I placed them in an album. Let me go get it." Mrs. Walsh left the room.

Randy glanced my way. "It seemed like you were in disbelief the night we discussed it." He smiled.

I almost blushed and felt apologetic, but who would be convinced of that? Mrs. Walsh walked back into the room.

"Here you go, dear."

Mrs. Walsh handed me the brochure. I began looking at the front, admiring the photo of St. Joseph's Church. I then opened it to read the inside of the pamphlet. I reached the bottom and continued to read. *Rebuilt in 1923*. I took a deep breath and handed the brochure to Randy to read.

"Look at the date."

Randy took the brochure and hunted for the date at the bottom. He grinned and began to describe in detail a few of the 23 stories with his mother. She listened and smiled too, but it was hard to tell what her thoughts were on the matter. We changed the subject, and then it was time to leave. Randy and I said our goodbyes, and off we went to San Francisco for dinner.

We got to the city, but it was difficult to find a parking place. Randy circled several corners with no luck.

"Gertie, we need you!" I exclaimed.

Randy stared peculiarly. "Who's Gertie?" he asked.

10: The Amazing Gertie and Advanced Spiritual Insights

"Gertie is one of my angels. One of her specialties is parking spots!"

"Are you kidding me?" Randy was now amused.

"Gertie, please, we need a close parking spot! Randy, please go back to the restaurant. We will find a perfect place to park the car."

Randy glanced over once more, puzzled.

"Okay. Let's try again!" Randy replied.

Randy and I drove right up to the restaurant. No parking spots. I inspected each side of the street. All of a sudden, someone pulled out right smack in front of the restaurant. Randy paused, acted pleasantly surprised, and pulled in.

"Thank you, Gertie!" I was pleased to show Randy the magic.

Randy chuckled, "Thank you, Gertie!"

We got out of the car and entered the restaurant. We were seated right away.

Randy curiously asked, "Did you ask Gertie to help us get a seat right away?"

"No." I grinned and was floored he even thought of asking such a question.

We ordered a drink.

"Cin, tell me more about Gertie."

"Sure. It's a miraculous story," I responded.

I began reflecting upon the beginning of the Gertie story. It had been awhile since I had repeated it to anyone and I was trying to put it together in my mind before sharing it with Randy.

Randy was getting comfortable in his seat. He took a menu and placed it in front of himself and started scanning it, then he stopped and looked up.

"I know what I want."

I wasn't very hungry or interested in looking at the full menu.

"Me too. I just want the soup special."

Randy took my menu, placed it on top of his, with a welcoming grin to begin.

"Well…about fourteen years ago or so, I went to a spiritual class and was introduced to a meditative technique to connect to my guardian angel. There were about ten women sitting in a circle, ready to begin the process. We started by imagining we were settled in the middle row in an empty theater. We were told there was a lever on the left side of one of the arms of the chair. This lever would open the plush red velvet theater curtain when we were ready to see our angel. Just as the curtain began to open, we needed to ask the angel their name.

"I sat there for only a few minutes with my eyes closed. While turning the lever, the plush velvet curtain was drawn. I opened my eyes and I asked my angel's name. There before me was an older woman with her hair pulled back in a bun, wearing an old-fashioned dress.

"My name is Gertie, she said. I closed my eyes tightly, pressed the lever on the arm rest, and the curtain closed. I quickly reopened it and hoped to see a beautiful young angel with white feathered wings appear. But there stood the older woman with an inviting smile. Perplexed, I again asked her name. She repeated, my name is Gertie.

"I thought I didn't get the assignment. I closed the curtain disappointed and unsure. When everyone came out of contemplation, the sharing began.

"I listened to the other ladies talk of names like Angelica, Felicia, Miciella, etc., with flowing dresses, golden locks, and angel wings. It was then my turn to narrate the experience.

"Gertie! I uttered. My angel's name is Gertie, and she's an elder. She was wearing an old-fashioned dress, and her hair was pulled back in a bun.

"I knew I had made a mistake. I was remarkably disturbed. No one saw anything remotely close to what I had witnessed that winter eve many years ago. As I attentively watched the women in the circle, a few chuckled, some were very amused, and other's expressions showed they weren't so sure I had gotten the assignment right either. The evening ended. I walked to my car shaking my head in disbelief. I was down on myself for a few days after that."

The waitress returned with our drinks.

"Cin, what a name: Gertie? It's such an old-fashioned name," Randy added.

"Yes, it is. I was considerably unsure about the entire experience. Something started to happen in the weeks following, though. I began hearing the names Gertie and Gertrude. What are the odds of this old-fashioned name appearing again in this ultra-modern world? I held onto the synchronicities and took notice that something was up with these signs.

"As the years unfolded, more came into light, and I became spiritually in tune. I began talking to Gertie, asking for assistance, especially for parking spaces and—oh my—she never failed to find a perfect parking spot! Just like this evening!"

Randy smiled.

"Others in my life started using Gertie, but I informed them that they had their own angels and it was important to access them. I didn't want her to get worn out! Gertie is still highly revered, especially by my young adult children."

Randy and I were both chuckling then.

"About eight years ago, I took a death and dying class. It was formally known as Compassion in Action, and now is The Twilight Brigade. I wanted it to become part of my life's work to assist people in transition. Dannion Brinkley, who had at least three near-death experiences, developed this heartfelt training weekend. It truly changed my life!"

"Dannion Brinkley? I never heard of him." Randy was eager to know more about the man.

"Dannion was a sniper in Vietnam, and part of his healing and work was to be of service to those who were dying. I don't know much about the Vietnam part, but the little I've learned was startling. In regards to his near-death experience, I believe the story goes like this. One day he was sitting on his couch in his living room talking on the phone, and a bolt of lightning reached straight into the phone line, struck and killed him. He was dead for twenty-eight minutes and was revived, which was a miracle in itself."

"What? How can someone be dead for twenty-eight minutes?" Randy was puzzled.

"I've come to trust there are many things we don't know unless we're up close to a similar situation. But there are thousands upon thousands of individuals who have had near-death experiences and are beginning to speak out, like Dannion. And me too."

"You too?"

"Yes. Another story for another time, Randy."

Randy lifted his brow with curiosity.

"Dannion then went to the other side, or heaven as most call it, and was told many events about his life and mission. He was even shown things that turned out to be true years later. Dannion returned to not only tell his story, but it also changed him so profoundly that he dedicated his life to helping people transition. Specifically our veterans, since many die alone."

"Wow, sounds like a profound man."

"Indeed."

The waitress emerged. Randy ordered our meals and refocused on me.

"Cin, this is better than any movie out there right now!"

"You haven't heard anything yet." I grinned.

11: Gertie Had a Mission

"In the months that passed after I took that wondrous death and dying class, I received a call from a Compassion in Action friend. He asked if it was possible for me to take over an assignment, helping an elder transition, because he had an emergency to attend. Back then, I was working two businesses and was worn out. I felt this unbelievable tingle up and down my spine. The nudges wouldn't let up. Nudges were a significant indicator when it was vital I pay attention or move forward on a pending situation. I was certain I needed to take the assignment.

"I was asked by Steven to call the coordinator, Nadia, and she would fill me in on the details. She was in charge of the northern California area for that organization. Nadia explained the details of my first assignment, including the fact that the elder was dying of stomach cancer. When she mentioned the elder's name, I was taken aback! Gertrude."

"Gertrude? Hmmm…"

"I asked if Gertrude's nickname was Gertie. Nadia didn't know. After I received all the information necessary, we ended our conversation, and I was extremely anxious to meet this Gertrude."

"Gertrude? What are the odds of that name showing up in your life again?" Randy interjected.

"Wild, isn't it? Just wait, there's so much more."

Randy paid close attention. He took a sip of his drink and was eager for me to continue.

"A few evenings passed, and I walked to Gertrude's hospital

71

room in anticipation. As I entered the room, there before me was the woman who showed up in my vision during the Guardian Angel meditation class, many years ago—but how in the world could this be? Angels were supposed to be in spirit."

"Cynthia, are you serious? This isn't for real." Randy laughed. "For real, Randy. For real." I smiled as I continued. "Gertie's hair was pulled back; her face was exactly how I remembered it when I was in the meditation class. I was absolutely stunned and all but paralyzed by this almost-paranormal meeting. I took a seat.

"As I sat there in complete and utter silence, it felt surreal watching Gertrude and her daughter converse. I thought I was in one of those parallel universes people talk about. "While they were busy with each other, I reviewed the meditation class experience in my mind, combing over every detail. I also took notice of the photos that surrounded Gertrude's small space: Mother Teresa, the Dalai Lama, and another Indian-looking guru. And then, a photo of Gertrude and her daughter.

"Gertrude was wearing the same style of dress I had seen in my vision. I took a deep breath and just sat there, numb."

"The same dress that was in your vision? Now you're scaring me," Randy said. "I don't remember the color, but I remember the style. Tell me about it!" I added. "The photos of the guru and Mother Teresa gave a sense of comfort that I could probably tell my story to her! I held on to this unimaginable secret for about four days. I then felt confident enough to share it with Gertrude the next evening.

"Has anyone ever called you Gertie?" Gertrude's face lit up

through the suffering, like a bright and shining star. "Only one other person called me by that name many years ago, dear. A man who was the love of my life!" she replied. "I took a cautious breath and proceeded to reveal my Gertie story to her. I fixedly gazed at her as I poured out my heart. She smiled steadily and nodded her head through the details and quietly waited. It was as if she had a special message.

"Please call me Gertie, dear. I am your angel. It was time for us to meet!" Randy was now shaking his head in disbelief. "My excitement amplified, Randy! I thought angels were not in a body. How was it possible?" I repeated, "How was it conceivable?" Randy was now on the edge of his seat waiting for more.

"I sat there wanting to ask her question after question, but I couldn't speak. My mind was running in numerous directions. I guess it was crucial to just be and take in this confusing experience. Gertie and I ended our evening. As I was driving home, I continued to hear in my mind, I am your angel, it was time to meet. I kept saying it over and over. How was it possible? I narrated it to a few friends the next day and they were as perplexed as I was."

"I've never heard of such a thing. But, believe it or not, I've not been aware of many of the things you've already shared since we remet! Cynthia Long, you are one fascinating person!"

"I don't know about fascinating. It's more like mainstream unusual!" I replied in a joking manner. "Steven returned, and we spent about a week more with Gertie before she passed on. We touched upon a myriad of feelings, memories of personal history, and the wisdom from her soul. I got to ask several questions, and she was very generous to answer, even when the pain of her cancer took over. I would ask Gertie to stop at times, witnessing her agony, but she insisted and continued. "One of the burning questions I asked Gertie was if she had anything significant to share that changed the course of her life for the better.

"Gertie thought about it and said, 'yes, it's about forgiveness. We must come to a place to forgive everyone who has ever hurt us. Forgive ourselves for those we have hurt. And try to heal the issues within and without."

Randy was paying rapt attention to my story. He asked a most curious question that I also had wondered about. "What does without mean? It sounds contradictory."

"Yes, I also had to stop and explore this term as it was unfamiliar. I never asked Gertie but because she was into the Eastern mystical traditions, it sounded like it came from one of the guru's teachings. My understanding, it's about healing what's outside of us. In this case, the person we're having a conflict with.

* * *

"Gertrude continued her story, stating at different points in her life that she thought forgiveness was not achievable. I was so invested in my own torment that forgiveness could never break through my stubbornness. But then, I had an epiphany after I had a conversation with someone very important. Forgiveness isn't about the other person, initially. It's about you and your healing. But if you want to reach higher on the forgiveness ladder, it can bring the higher-degree of *forgiving someone* up a notch to a greater degree of consciousness, if one can forgive on this level. Unfortunately, some won't ever reach the beginning stages of forgiveness.

"Gertie, I don't completely understand," I replied to her.

Gertie pondered. She reached up and took a long strand of hair from the tightly placed bun on her head and began twirling it. It was as if this quirk soothed her in some way. After a few seconds of twirling, Gertie continued.

"Let's take the example of someone I knew who lost her beautiful twenty-year-old daughter. She was kidnapped and killed by a man who was crazed on drugs. Joan, this young girl's mother, after too many difficult years of excruciating torment, searched high and low to get over that tragedy. She wanted closure but couldn't get there. Joan finally arrived at a place where she wanted to completely forgive this man for killing her beautiful child. After much contemplation, Joan wrote him a letter while he was in prison. She thought this would be the solution. And even when the man wrote back, it still didn't get her to a degree of peace Joan yearned for. She knew there was still more spiritual work to do. Joan then understood was integral to meet him, eye-to-eye, heart-to-heart.

"How difficult it must have been, but Joan had the courage to at least attempt to heal from such a tragedy. When the face-to-face meeting took place, intense tears were shed, and so many pent up feelings that were harming both of them were loosened and released. Tremendous healing was now possible. Joan finally let go of all her hurt and resentment. This day she was able to truly listen to this man's story— Joan was only invested in her own up to that point. It was necessary to hear its entirety to come to a compassionate place. The man also released the agonizing misery of taking a vibrant young woman's life—something that probably would have never happened if he hadn't been addicted to drugs."

"Yes, he made a tragic choice, for sure. I see what you mean now. There are many missing parts to lots of stories, I believe. How many people have only a part of the story, and how many are still in pain because of it?" I replied.

"Most people never look past their own pain or story. Stories can create judgment of others, especially one-sided stories, yet it's the story that provides the opportunity and can activate the forgiveness process. A story helps some to get there…or not. A choice one makes. The ultimate goal, though, for the two parties involved in the story is to learn, grow, and heal. On the highest level, a story isn't necessary."

I was deep in thought about this statement. I had never heard of this before. "Gertie, what do you mean, *on the highest level, a story isn't necessary?*" I asked, perplexed.

"Those who have reached this degree of understanding—they don't want or need to hear the story. They already know; people are where they're supposed to be. They understand that we are not just our body, our personality traits, and the choices we make. We are souls who have come here to evolve. Those who have chosen tough lessons will evolve faster, no doubt, if they learn, grow, and ultimately take the information and apply it in a useful manner."

"Very interesting…"

"Eventually, Joan began working in the prison system teaching inmates how to forgive. Out of tragedy, came a blessing. But this mother was willing and ready to reach another level of forgiveness. This was so extreme, few can reach it at this point."

I was breathless. I didn't know what to say to Gertie, as I had never heard anyone who forgave in that manner. To forgive someone who has murdered their child? That was unbelievable!

I reflected again. "Gertie, isn't this what Christ's ministry was about?"

"Christ was a master teacher of the true meaning of unconditional love. Forgiveness is the ultimate pathway to true love."

"Yes." I nodded. "Gertie, I'm curious, who did you have this conversation with that helped you?"

"Christi, my daughter. Christi helped me in this process." Gertie floated off into the distance, her eyes tearing up.

* * *

"Cin, that is mind blowing!" Randy paused and contemplated.

"I'm now re-examining my own forgiveness issues," he said.

"Yes, most of us have them lurking around."

"There was one last thing Gertie was determined to make known. Have you had enough?"

"Cin, please go on. This is almost like a lifetime of therapy."

* * *

One evening when I arrived, Gertie was all propped up in her hospital bed, her hair neatly pulled back in her favorite bun style. It felt as though she was excitedly prepared to open up. I couldn't read her mannerisms exactly, but it appeared Gertie wanted to get started right away.

"Dear, there's something critically important I want you to begin to understand."

I took a seat, placed my purse down on the side of the worn, stuffed chair, and squirmed around to get in a comfortable position.

"What is it, Gertie?"

"Have you ever been in love? A love beyond anything you ever could imagine?" she asked. I didn't understand her point, or where Gertie was going with that question.

"Well, I was married for twenty years and thought I was in love. But it didn't feel like true love after awhile—couldn't have been. I don't believe true love ends," I replied to her.

"No, true love doesn't end, Cin." Gertie was then smiling affectionately. The dim twinkle in her tired, yet determined eyes was affecting me in a mystical way—almost as if Gertie wanted me to open up like never before. Soul-to-soul.

"Let me ask you in this manner. Go back to the events where you felt you were deeply in love. It's sometimes called the honeymoon stage." Gertie was hopeful I would absorb the lesson quickly by giving an example.

"Yes, I've had a few honeymoon-stage relationships. Looking back, my two-year courtship with my husband was a honeymoon stage. The twenty-year marriage had more of those moments when the children were small. After the divorce, I had a four-year relationship with a man, but we took a break from one another, and he supposedly found a new love. After a while, he wanted to come back, which I pondered, but then felt it wouldn't work." I slowly and thoughtfully replied in retrospect as I tried to recall.

"And when this stage ended, or better yet, that person left your life, how did you feel?" Gertie asked.

"I can say it was challenging. No one ever wants the romantic feeling to end. This kind of love is what everyone desires. Look at the romance industry; it's a billion dollar empire because it all boils down to the entire world desiring love," I replied.

I stopped briefly to recall more wondrous past moments. "I remember when my sweet, late aunt materialized in a corner of the hospital room where one of my elderly uncles had spent his last days. My late aunt was waiting for him to pass away so that she could take him home. When I told my aunt that I missed her, she opened her arms and enveloped every part of my body. It was like the love of heaven entered my entire being. It was that astounding. I actually almost fell off my chair while in tears. The love she sent was that powerful. I didn't want that feeling to end, Gertie."

"The birth and childhood stages of my children, who loved unconditionally and thought I was the greatest human on the planet, were fleeting but also profound. I also had elevated feelings of love when I went to heaven during my NDE. The NDE, though, felt similar to the honeymoon period of a relationship." I paused, my NDE thoughts popped out of my head and into the clouds of heaven. My body reacted intimately, breaking out in goose bumps. It was all a glorious remembering. Seconds later, new thoughts jumped back in my head, and I continued.

Gertie was observing my mannerisms.

"Oh, I forgot, there were a few times I had spiritual occurrences, and it was a heightened feeling as well."

"But for now, let's just talk about the breakup of a relationship

79

between two people. One withdrawing from the other."

"Okay," I hesitantly replied. I still wasn't sure where Gertie was going with this.

"When the other person withdrew his love, how did you feel?" she asked.

"Horrible. It was like my heart dropped into the pit of my stomach. I ached and couldn't function." Then I recalled a few such relationship episodes.

"And when we withdraw our love from another it's a different experience altogether, isn't it?" Gertie asked.

"Yes, of course." I readjusted my posture since I felt a little uneasy reminiscing about a few past connections I had left unfinished. "Reflecting back, one was a teenage relationship and another, my husband. He never wanted to sit down and talk about any issues during the marriage. I guess it was very uncomfortable. It always ended in an argument, with him storming out of the house. He didn't want to learn or work toward a better relationship."

Gertie courteously listened, then added, "True love between two people isn't just about the couple actually. It's about each person individually learning the intricacies to find true love within. This is an example of each soul indirectly assisting the other to get to this magical place, through the romance stage of a relationship. The key is to stay in this blessed place, if the other is present or if he or she has left the relationship, physically or emotionally. Humanity doesn't truly understand romance yet."

"I guess I don't understand romance either. Wow, Gertie, this would be a new concept for most."

"Romance is a trigger for what each person is capable of achieving within. Romance mostly ends because we feel it's the other party who is responsible for the demise of the relationship. That person has withdrawn their love, and they are supposedly making the other person experience a terrible heartbreak. So, when perceived love is withheld, or ends, it feels as if we're disconnected, and to reconnect, we assume we need another person, which is a facade.

"Have you ever met someone and immediately felt the sparks of attraction ignited? You knew somehow that this person was meant to be in your life and you instinctively wanted to be close, and you might have even thought that you could spend the rest of your life with that person?" Gertie's eyes were wide with excitement and all wound up. She obviously felt very strongly about this subject for some reason. It sounded like she experienced this attraction with the love of her life.

"I've felt glimpses of this, Gertie. I would love to be in the midst of such a feeling always. I'm fascinated by those who are still in love after many years. I know dozens of couples. I can only recollect one who is in love like that."

"That instinctive connection is clearly about one soul recognizing another from a different time and place. More often than not, the connection is so uncanny that it almost feels impossible, but it is all part of God's plan."

"Yes, Gertie. I'm reminded of a story of a woman whose husband left her for another. She was so miserable and couldn't function for months. One early morning, she decided to get in her car and just drive. She ended up at a roadside diner, a hundred miles from her home at three in the morning. She entered the diner and took a seat. There was a man who sat two stools over from her. The man noticed that she was

81

in a sad state and attempted to cheer her up. He began to engage her in a conversation. They ended up talking for hours. One thing led to another, and a year later she married him. She felt it was destiny that brought them together. They have been married for over thirty years now. If she hadn't gotten into her car that early morning hour and driven to that diner, would it have been a lost opportunity?"

"If it was meant to be, it could never be lost," Gertie responded.

"My cousin also had a heartbreaking experience. She was married to her first husband when she was only sixteen. He left her for another woman, when my cousin was in her forties. She was distressed for years. I felt and mentioned that there was someone else for her. I could just sense it, perhaps the love of her life. She was ambivalent, but a few years later, this special man walked into her life out of the blue. In retrospect, she saw it differently."

"Again, God always has a plan. Her time with her first husband was up, but given that she had no faith and trust in the greater plan, she suffered immensely, I imagine. Obviously, she didn't understand that true love isn't just about the other person. Her first husband's soul gave her the opportunity to learn this important lesson," Gertie responded.

"I still don't believe she gets the opportunity and true love part."

"For another time, my dear. If one goes out in the world and asks randomly about stories like the ones you've just narrated, there would be an endless supply of similar connections. Often times, those coupling for shorter durations need to have the experience of having children specifically for the lessons they will all learn along the way."

"I believe this too, Gertie."

"If humanity understood romance, practiced and lived this life lesson, there would be fewer breakups; more people would be in the state of "true love" and self-satisfied with a partner or without. It all begins within."

Gertie took a piece from her neatly bunned-up hair and began twirling it while in contemplation. Her kind, fatigued eyes held my attention.

"Sweet child, this is your life journey and yours alone. Every situation and person added into your life is for your growth. We are humans having a spiritual experience. We emerged from love, and love should be our natural state of being. Children inherently know this."

"Gertie, so what you are saying is that I should live as if I'm in romantic love even when I'm alone?" I still wasn't grasping the lesson she was trying to teach.

"Alone or not! The fact is, love can never be taken away. We give too much power to others and discount our own true nature. Cin, you must become quiet and learn to get to know your soul better. This in turn will help you to live with greater love in your life."

Gertie's tone was slowing down at that point. I knew it was necessary to end our conversation on this subject matter.

"I'm going to put this on the back burner for now; it's pretty advanced."

Gertie took a breath and responded firmly and convincingly. "Dear, take it in small doses. Once you get this understanding and live it, your life will change dramatically."

She paused and drifted off, holding her strand of hair. She refocused and carefully watched as I stood and prepared to leave.

"Cin, you must learn to meditate. It will be life changing."

"I took a class a few years back, but I still haven't incorporated meditation into my life."

I walked over, hugged her, and said my goodbyes. Our embrace was noticeably longer that evening. I felt we might be close to the end of our time together, which was distressing to imagine.

* * *

"Randy, it was very clear. I wasn't just there to help Gertie's transition. I was mainly there for her to reveal the insight I was destined to hear before she passed on. I was saddened that our connection was brief, but it was meant to be—in the human form, anyway. Her body was quickly fading, and her spirit was ready to soar."

"Yes, you were there for a bigger reason, for sure... I'm not getting the romance part. It's too far out there for me." Randy was noticeably uncomfortable.

"Likewise myself." I smiled with affection.

"Did you ever ask Gertie if she lived this sort of romantic state in her own life?"

"No, I just assumed she was far advanced into this stage. I was so taken by the concept and somewhat hypnotized, my mind was stuck and focused on my past relationships, which were all great examples of romantic disconnect."

I sat there in a melancholy state, reviewing my last statement. I was still in the same place emotionally as when Gertie and I had that last conversation on romantic love. Little had changed in that direction, except that I took her advice and began meditating.

"Cin, are you okay?" asked Randy when he noticed my dispirited mood.

"I'm fine. For years I placed this entire lesson aside and am just reviewing it now. It reminded me of some aching circumstances."

I took a breath. "Gertie passed away not too long after Steven returned. I attended her small funeral service. I went on with my life. But then…"

The waitress returned with our meal. She placed our plates in front of us and we picked up our utensils.

"Cin, please continue."

"Randy, let's talk about this another time."

We finished our meal in silence.

"Cin, you're awfully quiet. Did I say something to offend you?"

"Not at all. I get this way every so often."

We left the restaurant and Randy drove straight for my car. We got out. Randy asked for my keys, opened the driver's door, ushered me inside, and gave a heartfelt hug.

"Thank you for the pleasant evening. I'll call you tomorrow."

"Okay. Thank you for listening. Hope it wasn't too uncomfortable?"

"Not at all. Cannot wait to hear the rest."

* * *

On the way home from Randy's, I recalled the synchronicities between Christi and I, months after Gertie's passing. One day while I was driving to Los Altos, I remembered that it was important to stop at the bank—a task I'd put off that week. Impatiently standing in line, I noticed Gertie's daughter, Christi. I got her attention but she didn't make a connection at first. We conversed for a few minutes and both went on our separate ways. I didn't feel it was unusual, and I went on with my life.

A year or more later, I placed an ad in the newspaper for my services as a personal assistant because I needed more clients—the Bay Area was populated by well over a million people. One day, I picked up my phone messages to see if I had any potential clients. One person's voice stood out, and I was extremely curious if that was Gertie's daughter. I called the woman back and discovered it was Christi. At first it was challenging to understand that coincidence since she didn't know anything about me or my business. We were both amazed. We chatted away about insignificant topics until I got a nudge to unearth the following.

"Christi, there was a conversation I had with your mother before she passed. I forgot to mention it to you. Every so often I thought to myself, *Why didn't I mention this to Christi?* I know you would want to hear it. In my opinion, your mother has had a hand in connecting us once again. I asked your mother if there was anything that changed the course of her life and if she would be so kind to share."

Christi was silent and eager to hear.

"Gertie said we must forgive ourselves for those we have hurt. Forgive everyone who has ever hurt us, and make an effort to heal the situation."

"I assisted my mother in this process?" Christi began to tear up.

"Yes, it seems so."

"Years ago, my mother would become very still when I would mention forgiveness in any form or fashion. It now makes sense. She was obviously observing and perhaps taking the information to apply it to her own forgiveness issues."

I gave Christi space to digest and collect herself.

Christi mentioned that she was still trying to cope with her mother's death. I made some effort to comfort her after the news given. We ended our conversation, and life went on until the next synchronicity with Christi.

It occurred during a church seminar from the previous year. I had been sitting among fifty or so people scattered here and there throughout the church. A speaker had just finished up, and we had a short break. I began talking with a man sitting close by, and the topic of angels surfaced. I felt a need to tell him about my Gertie story. As I was reminiscing, minutes later I sensed that someone had sat right behind my chair while I was sharing the uncanny synchronicities of the encounter. I turned around after I was finished, and who was in back of me? Gertie's daughter, Christi! We jumped up, hugged each other, almost screaming in excitement, but didn't want to disturb the other participants and held back. We were both shaken by this paranormal occurrence. Words like *unbelievable, unreal* and *incredible* came tumbling out of our quivering mouths. It took awhile for us to compose ourselves. The intriguing part was when Christi mentioned that she still struggled with Gertie's death and felt pushed to go to this event, but there were so many obstacles placed in her way, she wondered why she kept feeling hard-pressed to go. When Christi's eyes met mine, she automatically knew why. She made it a point to mention that next Sunday was Gertie's third-year death anniversary, which was just a week away. I was honored to be invited.

There probably were hundreds of churches among a million people in the San Jose area. Christi began attending this church not too long ago, which was a fair distance from where she lived. She could have chosen to sit in any of the dozens of empty seats and spaces, but right behind me was where she was probably led to sit. I could have also chose another topic to talk about. Gertie is simply amazing!

I then went to another memory of Christi a few years later. I was in my car one morning listening to a spiritual program. I was so busy during that peak work time, that tuning into this station was a rarity. I began zooming in on the interview in progress and I was taken back as I was almost sure that it was Gertie's daughter, Christi, being interviewed. I waited with anticipation to hear her name. Minutes later, a confirmation—indeed it was Christi! It was totally off the charts! It was probably a reminder that Gertie was right by my side.

I reached the driveway and went to bed.

A Few Days Later

The doorbell rang. I opened it to find a bouquet of flowers and card.

You are the best thing that ever happened to me.

Thank you for being in my life.

Randy

I was beginning to melt. I did not want to melt. I still wasn't sure. I had one foot in and one foot out of the relationship. *Help me, God! Dear God, I need help!*

Deep breathing was beginning to be habitual, and meditation was becoming part of my life (finally!). I braced myself, breathing in and out. I waited to calm down. While I dialed Randy's number, I was puzzled as to why I was reacting like that.

"Thank you for the gift of flowers. It was very nice of you."

"No one has ever touched my life like you. I'm the luckiest man in the world!"

"You are a very kind and thoughtful man."

We talked a bit and hung up.

After I ended the call, I placed the flowers in a vase. I continued to have thoughts of why I had these awkward feelings—guessing there must be more to it than I could understand. I walked over to the computer room. Halfway there, I began to get unusually dizzy and almost went into a panic attack. I folded my arms across my chest. I felt as if I might faint. My mother didn't know what to do.

"Are you okay? What's going on? Maybe a Valium would help you?"

She helped me into my bedroom to lie down.

I closed my eyes, and I could clearly see Randy in Oakland driving somewhere. Maybe he was going to get robbed or hurt? He didn't mention where he was when I called. I thought about calling back to warn him, but I feared maybe he'd feel I was a bit weird. It was too early to discuss the deeper part of my spiritual side. My mother handed me a Valium; I took only half. I didn't usually take calming medications, but this was off a scary experience. The feelings subsided, and I fell asleep. That night Randy called.

"Hi, sweetie. Hope you had a good day?" Randy was his normal, happy, go-lucky self.

"It was sort of bizarre. Were you in Oakland today?" I was curious.

Nothing but silence… "Wow, yes, how did you know?"

"I just felt you were there. Are you okay? I was a bit worried."

"I'm fine. Sort of weird that you knew I was in Oakland."

"Yes, it was somewhat of a strange experience." Mulling over it and almost laughing to myself, *Strange to some people maybe!*

"Hey, why don't you come up to my place for the weekend? I'll cook dinner for us. We'll watch a movie and just hang out. You can sleep in my bed, and I'll sleep in the guest room."

Now, I was the one who was quiet. *Hmmm… Will he sleep in the other room?*

"Cin… Cin… You're quiet… I promise to be a gentleman."

"Okay."

"Great. We can talk more about it before next weekend."

"Okay."

I changed the subject. "Last weekend my friend's house burned down. I just heard about it today. She lost everything. I want to help in some way."

"I have a friend, actually an ex-coworker whose house burned down in the Oakland fire. He was on the bay, sailing. He watched his home and the surroundings incinerate to the ground from his boat. The only thing he had left were the small boat and clothes on his back. At work we gave him a shower," Randy said.

"What a great idea! So you understand?"

"Yes, I do understand. I'd like to contribute to your friend's cause too."

I listened to his heartfelt words and took him up on his offer to assist.

We got off the phone, and I didn't know why I had such an attack. Another back-burner situation—a place I put some things that don't make sense, but usually is a puzzle piece for something far greater.

I drove up to Randy's home in the late afternoon on Friday, but not without another 23 sighting. I called Jen on the way to update her on the new man in my life. We were pretty heavily engaged in conversation when an old, rickety truck with splintery wooden sides abruptly turned into my lane. I'd taken my eyes off the road for only a few seconds, but when I looked back up, I screamed bloody murder and slammed on my brakes.

"Cin, are you okay?" Jen cried out.

I went silent. I had an eerie feeling as I watched the truck in front of me.

"Jen, an old truck almost cut me off, and now I'm staring at the number 23 spray painted in black on the tailgate."

Jen was awe struck.

"Oh wow! How many times have you seen that number this last year?"

"Almost every day!"

And then, Jen was silent.

"Jen, are you there? Jen? Jen?"

"Oh my God! I just glanced over at the TV and there's this woman race car driver standing next to her car. Guess what the number is?"

I was again silent.

"23!"

"What?"

Jen and I were almost beside ourselves.

"What do you feel all this means, Cin?"

"I don't know. This number has been following me ever since Jonathan mentioned it!"

"For sure it's calling for your attention and maybe mine too!" Jen said in a matter-of-fact manner as we ended the call, and I proceeded to drive to Randy's home.

As I reached the gate, I called Randy to buzz me in.

We met at my car and he mentioned that he needed groceries. I got out and moved toward the passenger door of his car. He moved around swiftly; his gentleman behavior was now set in stone.

As we were approaching the grocery store, there was a homeless man standing close to the entrance asking for money. As Randy and I passed him, I said, "I bless your way."

Randy curiously asked, "You bless his way?"

"Yes. Whenever I see a homeless person, I bless their way. They have chosen such a challenging life path. Blessing their way is honoring and asking for good things to come to them."

Randy looked at me and smiled. He grabbed a grocery cart, and

I followed beside him.

Randy chose an aisle, and when we were halfway down, he paused and turned. Taking me in his arms, he began dancing and singing to the piped music in the store. People were amused as they passed by. We embraced and continued our shopping.

"You are a charming and creative man, Randy Walsh!"

"You're a gift to me, Cin."

I stood there in wonderment.

As we checked out, the grocery bill totaled $32.23. Randy handed me the receipt and said, "Add this to your collection of stories!" I again smiled and we walked out of the store, and I placed the receipt in my purse.

We were almost at Randy's house when I noticed a dead dog on the side of the road. "Go to the light! Go to the light!" I whispered. Randy was now puzzled.

"Now what does that mean, Cin?"

"It's like a boost to get them to go to God's light. Usually animals know how to go to the light, but I want to make sure. Humans on the other hand, need assistance."

"Wow, I've never heard of that."

"I remember returning from one of my client's a few years back. She lived in the San Jose foothills. As I was driving down one of the steep hills, a motorcycle lost control three cars ahead of me and spun out. I noticed that the young man was lying on the road. I was going to stop, but there were people on the other side running over to him and his bike. It almost looked like he was staring at me while I passed. I knew he would not make it. I silently told him to go to the light. Even though it wasn't bloody gory, I've never witnessed anything remotely close to such a tragedy."

"I cannot imagine, Cin. Randy said softly."

12: Twenty-Three: The Romance Begins

"What happened to the young man in the accident?" Randy asked.

"The next day, I went looking for a newspaper to find out more information. He died immediately. He may have been transitioning when I guided him. He was 23 years old."

"23 years old?" Randy shook his head since this number kept appearing in stories.

"There's a responsibility for those of us who are spiritually awake to show the way to those leaving. It's part of our service to humanity."

Randy was quiet and very touched by this. He grabbed my hand and kissed it.

"I was extremely bothered by that incident for a few months. The young man's family planted a rose bush in the vicinity of the accident. It was a reminder to me, to others, and a memory for the family. Each week I drove by, I blessed his family and asked God to help them heal. To lose a child is the most devastating life experience one can go through, I'm sure. I almost lost my youngest son when he was three and a half. He was run over by a semi-truck driven by a young man who worked for our family. The driver was not paying attention and severely injured my sweet child. Jonathan spent a month in the hospital. We came very close to losing him."

"I'm sorry, Cin. It must have been very difficult to cope."

"I was far removed from my faith, but this incident was the catalyst to help wake me up spiritually. I was literally on my knees asking God for help.

"That was the era of John Bradshaw. He was very big on the dysfunctional family, the wounded child, and the roles each family member plays in the family system. I remember John describing role playing with the infamous mobile he made popular with figures of each family member, which helped me make sense out of all the family craziness. His work encouraged millions to begin healing their childhood pasts. I was one of the many wounded adult children. I'll tell you more about that experience later on."

We got back to Randy's home and began cooking our meal, which was an enjoyable diversion. We danced some more, laughed, ate a delicious meal, and watched movies. It was getting late, and I headed out with a big thank you and a hug. Randy was starting to become a big part of my life.

As I was driving home and listening to *Delilah, The Love Song Lady*, someone called into her show and mentioned he'd been dating this remarkable woman for 23 months. Delilah said, "It's very unusual for a man to remember dating a woman to the very month."

Amused, I continued my journey home.

The following weekend, Randy wanted me to drive to his place again since my friend Beth, whose home burned down, lived closer to Randy. We both had gifts for her.

We drove to Beth's temporary home. I purchased things I knew would be useful and handed her the gifts as we were welcomed into the home. Beth was astounded with emotion, and tears welled up in her eyes. She hugged each of us.

"Randy, I've heard a lot about you." He was impressed to hear I'd been talking about him with one of my friends.

"Cynthia, you are very fortunate to have someone like Randy in your life," Beth said in a bold manner. That was Beth's style. Once in awhile she caught people off guard, but she was the type of friend who would swim the ocean if I went missing.

With a steady gaze through her tears, Beth said, "Don't ever hurt her. She's very special!"

Randy was startled by that statement and eagerly replied, "Not in a million years!"

Our eyes fondly met.

After a pleasant afternoon with Beth, we stopped off at the store on our way back to Randy's house. Again, we were walking down the aisle, he took me in his arms, and began dancing and singing to the music. A couple walked up to us and asked us how long we had been married.

"Uhhh… Do we really look married? Do married couples do such things?"

Randy responded, "I wish."

I stepped back to look in. "I'm not ready for that yet!"

The husband and wife told us they were approaching 23 years of marriage, and they danced randomly, here and there, and felt they were unique. Randy and I glanced at each other and laughed. We apologized, not wanting them to presume we were laughing at them. Randy proceeded to tell the couple that the number 23 held a very significant meaning in my life.

Randy opened up to a few "23 stories," and the couple was amused with it all. We shook their hands, offered our names, and walked on. Randy led me to the plant and flower area. The woman there knew him.

"Hi, Randy."

"Hi, Jerri. This is Cynthia."

"Cynthia? The Cynthia I hear about each week when purchasing flowers?"

"Yes, this is the one—the Cynthia of my dreams."

"Nice to meet you, Jerri." I cast a glance at Jerri and then at Randy.

"Yes, finally nice to meet you, Cynthia. He's sure crazy about you!"

My eyes were still focused on Randy. He was smiling like he was sitting on top of the world.

Randy chose a beautiful arrangement, and we checked out.

"Thank you for the lovely flowers, Randy. Jerri appears to know you well?"

"You're welcome. Yes, Jerri loves to hear the updates of our relationship," Randy replied.

I was grateful for his generosity, but a small part of me wondered if this was for real or a dream? It was almost too perfect.

We had another lovely dinner and watched a movie. I was lying very comfortably on the couch. Randy was sitting on his leather chair enjoying the end of the movie.

"I must go home. I'm fading." I began gathering my things, still half asleep.

Randy noticed my cozy state. He got up from his leather chair, picked up the flowers he had purchased, handed them to me, and thanked me for a wonderful day. We walked out to my car. Randy asked for my keys, opened the car door, helped me in, and closed it.

As I was driving home, I started second guessing my feelings.

Am I shallow? Don't we need to have chemistry? Maybe love takes awhile to develop a physical chemistry? Damn! How can I be this confused at forty-nine years old?

* * *

The next weekend I was invited to stay at Randy's home, and it was enjoyable. We began talking about our family's Irish roots.

I mentioned that my dad loved his Irish heritage, and when my siblings and I were small, he would sing Irish songs and other old, family favorites. It was a very special memory. I also carried on the tradition and sang to my children.

"What songs did you sing?"

I thought about the names but couldn't recall any of the titles at first. I then remembered a few. "A favorite was *When Irish Eyes Are Smiling* and *Molly Malone*. Another, not Irish, *Side by Side*."

Randy peered with that same borderline-scared look that I noticed at the restaurant earlier on when I told him about St. Joseph's Church. I waited for him to speak.

"That's a favorite of my family's too."

That was odd. It wasn't even an Irish song. What in the world was going on? I was beginning to feel like my angels were pushing me into a serious relationship with him. I'd never had so many coincidences like this happen before. Synchronicities and my soul pulling at my heart strings!

The weekend went well. As always, he was a gentleman. Randy also kept his word. He slept in the guest bedroom the entire weekend. We were heading for the six-month point in our relationship. I was learning to look more at Randy's heart. Wasn't that what truly mattered? I was convinced that something bigger was at play here and just maybe my soul was taking me on a journey. So many signs smacking me in the face, almost screaming to get my attention, *This is your future, Cindy!* But I just didn't quite feel it. So, I went with the flow of life that handed me such a special man. With each passing day, he became my dearest friend, and I hoped that one day I might reminisce and truly see what the universe was trying to convey.

Another weekend drew near. Randy asked me to stay since we were going to a friend's house for dinner near his home.

That Friday, as had become my new habit, I started walking toward his bedroom to settle in. There was a beautiful package on the bed with a large card that had my name on it. I opened the card and truly melted by the thoughtful choosing. It was filled with kind and gentle words. At the bottom of the card in his own perfect penmanship, it read:

I'm glad we found each other.

I've been waiting for you all of my life!

I opened the gift, a beautiful two-piece, red gown and robe. *I'm done!* I never thought this would happen. Not in this lifetime. I turned immediately, and he was right behind me. I nearly jumped out of my skin! He must have stood there the entire time.

Randy and I embraced.

"Cin, you deserve to be spoiled. I'm here to change what were challenges into blessings."

I gently pulled away, again believing him.

It was such a safe feeling to finally find someone like Randy. I was sitting on cloud nine! The weekends rushed by—one by one, almost a blur. Some were intimate, while others were spent with his close friends and family—a few days here and there with my family and friends. The nights we just kicked back were welcomed—watching movies and having cozy dinners, dancing, and singing whenever and wherever.

One evening, I was helping Randy around his home and wanted to throw out the trash. I went to the garbage area, and there were two raccoons sifting through the refuse. I jumped back and yelped. They ran like the dickens and hopped over the fence. I was curious to know what raccoons symbolically meant and went back inside to look in my *Animal Speak Book* by Ted Andrews. It was a book I packed at that point because I wanted to know more about animals and their symbols. The Native Americans have kept this tradition alive. I scanned through the pages. I was most fascinated by the mask the raccoons wear. The book mentioned that the raccoon is associated with thievery. He is concealed behind a mask. He is an expert at disguise and secrecy. I looked up the number two, considering numbers also have symbolism. It read, "Feminine, dreams, cooperation." *Feminine, dreams, cooperation? Hmmm.* I then read the negative aspects, "Sensitivity and meddling." Two meant partnership. It piqued my curiosity. What this was really all about?

As I browsed at the bottom of the information, it said, "All double-digit numbers can be reduced to one of these nine aspects by adding the two digits together. For example, 23=2+3=5." I called out to Randy to read a few paragraphs. He was fascinated, especially with the example that used 23 since the author could have chosen any double digit, but he went with 23.

That evening, I had an unusual dream. The dream setting was in the outskirts of Georgia in the late 1800s. My father was a plantation owner. We lived in a white mansion, with a semi-wraparound porch—rockers and wicker chairs scattered around the perimeter. I had one sister. She was about fourteen, and I was probably around twelve. As I observed the dream, it was like I was standing outside of it. There was a knock at our front door. Our caretaker, Annie, a petite African American was straightening the beautifully decorated foyer. She walked over alone and opened the door to greet the caller since this was the proper thing to do in those days. My sister and I stood a foot or so behind Annie, looking to each side of her, studying the young man who was evidently courting my sister. I immediately noticed his white and brown two-toned convertible car sitting in the front driveway. I had never seen a car like that. As he was welcomed into our home, I caught a glimpse of his shoes, also two-toned of white and brown. I thought that to be very stylish, and I was also perplexed how he found shoes to match his car. Or was it a car to match his shoes?

I walked over and sat on the last stair of the winding staircase to eavesdrop. It felt as if he had frequented our home because Annie appeared comfortable with the situation. She asked William and my sister to follow her to the parlor. I watched them as they entered the over-stuffed room. My sister left the door open, barely a crack. It was not allowed by our father to close the door completely. Even a crack was forbidden, but she pushed the limits, especially with this young man, William, in her life. I sensed my sister was never this fearless before. I felt that the young man was the instigator. And he played the part as he peered at me in a mischievous manner through the crack in the door.

My father rushed down the staircase and asked who was in our home.

"William!" I exclaimed.

He abruptly barged into the parlor, pushing the door so hard it hit the back of the wall. He was annoyed about the door rules not being honored. William stood and spouted niceties. My father half-listened. William was trying to "butter him up." There was a response, but I couldn't hear what was said. I noticed that my father studied William from head to toe, shook his hand, turned away to search for a chair in the crowded room, placed it in front of the opened door, and then left the room. My sister acted flustered and turned to William and noticed his ashamed reaction. They both dropped their eyes down to the wooden planked floor, embarrassed, as my father stomped out of the room.

He passed by making a B-line for the kitchen. "I do not trust anyone with two-toned shoes. Keep an eye on your sister!"

I got up and walked over to the now opened door and peeked inside. My sister's back was sideways to the door. William caught me snooping and smiled. He noticed that I was considerably uncomfortable. I stepped back, turned, and proceeded to escape to the tree-lined lake on our property. It took a good five minutes of fast walking. It felt like I went there often for comfort and solace. I walked along the water's edge and finally found a soft, inviting place to sit. I was observing the ducks and other birds and began tossing pebbles into the water. Not more than twenty minutes went by when I heard twigs crackle and snap from behind. I suddenly turned and there was William, my sister's friend, standing with another mischievous smirk on his face. I was startled and stood abruptly. He graciously asked me to sit and talk. I was polite and sat down.

"I've wanted to talk to you for awhile. Would you be interested in a young man like me?" I took a quick glance down at his two-toned shined shoes, not to put any emphasis on them, and then up at him.

"My sister is in love with you," I cried out, disturbed.

He had this piercing look, like he was in love with me.

"Well, she'll get over it, don't you agree?"

I suddenly sat up in bed. What in the world was that about? I nudged Randy. He turned over, stretched a bit and yawned. I then recounted the dream.

"You are a very unique person, Cynthia Long."

"Yes, my father used to say they broke the mold when I was born!" I half laughed. We got up and began making breakfast. We talked, laughed, and danced in between preparing our meal. We fixed our plates and sat out on the patio to enjoy the grassy rolling hills.

The day went by quickly like most days did then. We decided to watch the sunrise the next morning and thought to drive to Oakland Hills, so we retired before 9:00 that evening to get an early start.

Before we went to sleep, I felt a presence in the corner of the room while Randy and I were reading. I stopped, put my book down, abruptly sprung up, and followed the energy pattern. Randy keenly noticed. He then set his book on his belly and watched the area I was focused on. I asked if he could see it.

"No. I don't see anything."

"Keep looking. There are times when I don't see anything, and then it moves. It's an energy. It's sort of wavy, like when one is driving on a hot day, and heat is rising off the road.

He continued to examine the alleged energy, almost like he was trying to concentrate on it. He suddenly stiffened and didn't move an inch.

"Don't concentrate. Just observe."

He did as I said and still, nothing.

"Cin, how do you do this?"

"Randy, I don't know. It just happened all of a sudden. I was told that on both sides of my family, there were aunts who were blessed with these gifts. I also feel that when I had a near-death experience as a child, it stimulated those gifts. It's been written about people who have had near-death experiences, there's a shift in the brain function."

Randy was in contemplation.

"So, do you believe I'm weird? Most mainstream people take issue with such things." I asked in uncertainty.

"No, I want to be able to see what you see. Can you teach me?"

"Honestly, no one taught me. I was self-taught."

"Do you feel comfortable sharing the NDE? I'm fascinated," Randy asked.

"Well, let's see. I haven't opened up about this story in years." I paused.

"I was about eight years old. My family drove to Santa Cruz to spend the day at the beach with friends. My mother asked this young girl, who was the daughter of my father's friend, to watch me while I was wading in the ocean. Lia was only about twelve years old. She and I began playing along the shore. I somehow slipped and was taken out to sea by a riptide, and tossed around in the water. I fought for breath for awhile, and then I had no more strength. I was like a limp rag doll. I gave up, exhausted. Everything around me went into slow motion, including my body movements. All of a sudden I could breathe, and it felt like I was free. I took in a big breath; no water entered my lungs. Air was plentiful. Almost like an elixir. The more I took in, the more I felt like the elixir was filling my entire body with pure love and a peace beyond any understanding.

"I turned and noticed dozens of beautiful fish circling my body. The colors were truly magnificent and over and above anything I had ever seen in my life. I also had the distinct feeling that the fish knew me somehow—that they were there to assist in some way. I was a part of them and they a part of me. It was puzzling at first.

"Beautiful, angelic music played. The melody was breathtaking. I had never heard anything like it before and have been searching for a similar experience ever since.

"My eyes were suddenly drawn to a small pin-size, vibrating, white light far in the distance. It began growing in size. As it expanded, the intricate harmonics flourished and were stimulating to where I was moved to tears. I then noticed a ghost-like figure of a woman in the spirited light. As I focused further, I intuitively knew she was not from this earth. The white light surrounding her pulsated in harmony with the music. It was as if the entire scene was in sync. She gently waved for me to come closer. I was mysteriously drawn to this woman and started swimming in a relaxed motion toward her. As I moved closer, she became familiar.

"I followed this lady's lead as the bright light turned into a swirling tunnel. As soon as we entered this phenomenon, it took only seconds to move through it. After the tunnel, we entered a paradise. I felt I had been to this place before. There, I encountered my grandfather, my uncle, some aunts, and other people I knew, but did not know why or how I recognized them. There was an intuitive understanding, a knowing. They were close to me, like family, and had been forever. More and more people gathered. I witnessed other angelic-type beings. They didn't have wings like religions have taught. They had this beautiful light surrounding them though. And everyone was youthful looking."

"What do you mean *they had this beautiful light surrounding them*?" Randy was curious.

"Well, there are depictions of halos in religious photographs that are sort of like what I witnessed. But this luminous light surrounded their entire being."

"Fascinating…"

I waited to see if Randy was going to ask any more questions, but none came forth.

I continued, "So, encapsulating love enveloped and poured out of everyone present. This astonishing sensation embraced every part of my body, mind, and spirit. I felt I was finally home. I was welcomed and deeply loved far greater than I had experienced on earth. I was not judged. I was honored and adored. I wanted to desperately remain in the presence of those who loved me like no other, and bask forever in the beautiful utopia. I was told that my life was not over and I should return to earth because I had a mission to accomplish. I was confused and extremely saddened. I did not want to go back, Randy.

"I thought about my family life. My father drank and often physically abused my mother. Part of my father's Irish roots were family brawls. He carried the tradition. My mother was gravely ill for much of my childhood. She was in and out of a sick bed—in the hospital and far removed due to the abuse, too many instances to count. I was the eldest daughter of five and had tremendous responsibility. I was overwhelmed as a child since there were many obligations to tend to when my mother was ill. My parents depended a great deal upon me.

"I had felt mostly alone and confused, but now I was in the presence of pure love. Anyone in their right mind would never want to return to a childhood nightmare like that. I was then shown—on a large screen—happy, future moments of my family for a purpose. My father was a kind and thoughtful man when he didn't drink. He was a baseball coach and took kids without fathers under his wing. The angels revealed occasions when my dad took me shopping for my future high school prom or other occasions for formal dresses. There was a scene where he insisted on matching shoes and a purse. My dad was there for me when alcohol wasn't a diversion. For a few minutes, I felt special that Daddy cared, was attentive and genuinely interested in assisting me.

"We would have other distinct future times together where we talked about the philosophy of life. Daddy was introspective. I would come to love that about him." I had an instant recollection, took a breath, and continued on.

"I suddenly remember the Angels shined a light on my father's real self. Alcohol addiction was a symptom of buried pain that he could not overcome. It was easier to desensitize. I was shown times I judged my father and I was immediately affected emotionally. The Angels mentioned these scenes were purposeful, only an introduction, and that there was more learning to come. A portion was somewhat memorable, touching and to view the future was unimaginable! I refocused on the assemblage. All those present in the large marbled room I suddenly found myself in were concentrated on me. I begged to stay since the meaningful events on earth I was shown were sporadic!"

"I have so many questions. Where to begin? Hmmm. So, you're saying that you automatically knew these thoughts and feelings?" Randy was very interested in the subject.

"Yes, communication was telepathic. I was shown different scenarios on the large movie screen. It's difficult to explain, but that is the best way to describe the experience."

"What is pure love?" Randy asked.

"Hmmm, how can I explain it? We have glimpses of this state of consciousness here on earth. Many call it unconditional love. Babies and children come from this place, and so do dogs. The feeling is an incredibly heightened emotion, like being in love. It's orgasmic in nature, but not sexual. Every square inch of your being is affected, which is a normal state in heaven." I shivered just recalling the phenomenon. "It's an extraordinary life event that one cannot wrap a human mind around. I just know that I want to experience this feeling every day of my life. It's that miraculous."

"Simply amazing! What do you mean, the angels revealed your father's real self?"

"I judged my father terribly growing up when he created havoc. But I didn't have the tools to understand that his horrible behavior was a systematic disconnect. It wasn't who he really was. When Dad went on a rampage, I couldn't relate until an idea came to me- to separate the night behavior from the day behavior. The day self was a kind and thoughtful human. But even then, it was challenging because the abuse was on going. It was difficult to even function normally, sometimes on a daily basis. My mother, siblings, and I were on emotional overload. It's taken years and experiences to get through it, and I still have some problems loving another unconditionally whose behavior is over the top- but at least I have more tools. Through the experiences with my father, the angels first introduced the virtue of looking at others' hearts and not only my own. I've been tested and re-tested and still have work to do."

"You totally forgave your father?"

"Yes, I totally forgave my father." I responded.

"I don't know if I could ever forgive a cruelty like this. Especially when it involves children." Randy's clearly disturbed.

"Look back to what Gertie shared about Joan forgiving the man who murdered her child? How and where did she get the strength to get to this place?" I add.

"I don't know."

"There something much bigger at play here, Randy. We just need to tap into it." Randy didn't respond. I carried on with my story.

"While I was in this library of sorts, those present introduced an ancient scroll that was laid out on a long, carved table. It revealed how my life and ultimate mission was going to unfold further."

"I'm going to do *this*? I asked. Suddenly there was another group in the room. I thought it was remarkable since they were not there only seconds before. There were telepathic nods from those present. I suddenly noticed a refined man in the corner. I recognized him some-how. I wanted to learn more, but it was like I was blocked from knowing anything about him. He wore a suit from the 1920s. He was very hand-some, manicured from head to toe, sporting a well-groomed mustache. The stately man was a devoted part of this gathering, and in some way had a part to play in my life. I got distracted by his attentiveness as he took in every detail. I was mesmerized by his shining eyes. Caught by the magnetism, he took notice, smiled, and telepathically communi-cated for me to pay attention to this meeting. As the group continued to reveal my life plan, I took a backseat to this phenomenal place. I was sure this was my home, and earth was a place I didn't want to be."

"I interrupted and said, 'I don't want to go back there.' I pleaded and began to cry."

"One of them gently said, 'Cynthia, you have a lot of work to do. And your biggest mission will not begin until you are much older."

"I felt heartbroken. The angels also presented me a scene when I was a teenager going through a magazine while sitting on the floor in my bedroom. I questioned what that had to do with anything, and then I came upon two beautiful children who had big, brown, wondrous eyes. I knew this little girl and boy were my future children. The angels men-tioned a third child, but the soul had not yet decided if he wanted to be part of my future family unit. The other two had made commitments. They mentioned that one of my sons would have a very big mission to accomplish.

"I attentively listened. In an odd way I understood it to be true, but this blessed place kept pulling on my heart strings. I kept remem-bering my chaotic family life. I chronicled everything and everyone around me.

"Again, the angels could read my mind, and then miraculously I could read all of theirs at once. That alone was mind blowing! An angel said, 'We sympathize with your deep and pain-filled feelings, but you will get through this. We promise. You should go back for greater reasons than what you can understand right now, but you must make the ultimate decision, Cynthia. It is your decision alone, dear child.'"

Randy hardly moved. I didn't know what he was thinking after I had unloaded so much on him. I wondered and waited. "Cin, the angels told of your future children? And you have three children. I've never heard anything like that before!"

"Yes. I now understand why Johnathan's soul was undecided."

I paused. "The weird part—I forgot about this portion in the life review while in Heaven—when I was sixteen, I was sitting on the floor in my bedroom and thumbing through a teen magazine. There in front of me were the two children I had witnessed during my life review. It was absolutely unnerving! I kept closing the magazine and then flipping to the page again, guessing I wasn't actually seeing it and speculating whether I was in my right mind."

"Weird part? You've shared so many wild stories. I'm beginning to wonder, am I dreaming? It's all so unreal." Randy was a bit spooked.

"Do you want me to change the subject?" I asked. "Are you kidding?" he grinned. "I got this far without running away!"

I laughed, and, at that instant, my mind disconnected far off somewhere, drifted away from Randy. I was re-living the last comment.

I snapped back, "To this day, I cannot remember all of what the angels revealed. Only what I've conveyed right now. For now, it's all unfolding like it should, I guess."

"Did you ever find out about the well-groomed mustached man in the suit?"

"No, I have no other information about him."

I noticed that Randy was wandering away from the conversation now.

"Randy, there are books on NDEs. It's probably due to the fact it hasn't interested you, and you never met anyone who has had this experience."

"No, it interests me."

"Well, maybe you had to hear this story for you to explore more. Anyway, all of a sudden I was slammed back into my body. According to Lia, a huge man pulled my near-lifeless body from the ocean by my long, tangled hair."

I stopped to collect my thoughts. "I barely remembered the man tugging at my hair. But I do somewhat remember how he carefully laid me on the ground along the shore. I violently coughed up salt water, spewing it from my mouth and nose. My eyes were filled with gritty sand. A crowd gathered. One guy stepped up, rolled me on my side, and began hitting my back as I began to dry heave. My parents had no clue what was happening. Later I found out that Lia had run to get them. By then, there were many people surrounding me. I finally was helped to a sitting position.

"I felt very ill. I could hardly see given that the sand was caked in and on my stinging eyes. I sensed sand entering every part of my body. I reached for my sand-encrusted, plugged ears. They immediately began to itch. I tried to relieve them; the area was now raw. But then I was stinging from another discomfort. I felt sand between my fingers. I took one hand and brushed the crevices. I touched my long strands of terribly matted hair. As I reached for my scalp, tiny morsels were stuck together. I ran my hand up and down the clumped strands crowding the edge of my face.

"I proceeded to my nose and ran my hand over my nostrils. Again, the same. It was as if I had an almost hopeless situation. While sitting, my rear began to itch. I could feel sand and more sand inside my bathing suit. I started remembering the ordeal of being tossed among the waves, but began contemplating how I captured so much sand in and on my body."

"Oh my Lord! I've never thought about how sand could end up in so many places. I bet you were fearful of the ocean after that ordeal?"

"It actually had the opposite effect," I answered.

"Where in the world were your parents?" Randy exclaimed.

"I heard my parents' panicked voices. My mother made her way over and began scolding Lia. Even though I was extremely exhausted and hurting, I felt bad for Lia. She was only twelve. She shouldn't have been in charge, especially around a moving and unpredictable large body of water. My father stooped down, brought me close to himself and asked all sorts of questions that I have no memory of."

I observed Randy. I could tell he was thoughtfully listening and analyzing every word I said, almost hypnotized by the story.

"What was so odd, was that the large man who had rescued me, had surprisingly disappeared. My father searched the surrounding area and asked several people because he wanted to thank him. Not one person noticed this man except Lia. She described him as a giant with very big hands and feet. I recalled her characterizing the large man as she stood on her tip toes waving her expressive hands to the sky to demonstrate his massive size. I watched closely, through a small crack in one eye, as all those listening snickered and discounted her. No one believed Lia except me.

"I was helped up and guided to the family's large beach blanket to recover from this ordeal. My mother tended to my immediate needs, wiping and scraping all the sand from my sore body, beginning with my stinging eyes. She poured clear water straight into my eyes, carefully wiping them. Much of the sand ran off my face, but it felt like there was still more sand in my red, sore eyes. I complained to my mother, but she continued on to my hair. It was tightly knotted, and specks of sand coated the bunched strands, making it difficult for her to comb out. The only small salvation, my scalp was extremely tough, but even then, I cringed. Every part of my body hurt, even under my fingernails. Sand made its way everywhere and held me hostage. Whatever I did to remove sand in one area, wasn't enough. There were many more parts to reach and all were sharply calling.

"I noticed everyone else not paying attention. It was as if nothing much had occurred, which was peculiar. My brothers and the other children were off playing. Lia took off and then returned not wanting anything to do with me. I took it in a way that I was blamed for her scolding and for my near drowning. I now understand she was just a child, with no adult mentor to assist in this ordeal or any other. Sadly, Lia disappeared a lot in her life after that. Being discounted didn't end with this story. I realize now that she never felt worthy, and she allowed others to overpower and prey on her weaknesses. I now feel she just didn't have the inner strength to overcome those who were mean spirited and permitted others to define her."

Randy wisely commented, "Back then parents did the best they knew how. There was little self-help guidance. What was available was expensive, and only some of the wealthy accepted it. Most old-timers had limited views and were resistant to learning anything new."

"I get it now, but it took awhile. I've come to realize, the more dysfunction, the more resistance," I added.

"Are you still in touch with Lia?" Randy curiously asked.

"No, our family has lost touch with Lia and her family" I sat there reflecting on where Lia was at this point in her life, especially emotionally.

"My father, his friend, and his wife were standing not far, laughing and drinking their ice-cold beers. I sat quietly watching as my mother continued to get me cleaned up. She was short-tempered and impatient due to my flinching, screeching, and at one point, crying. I was fed up with her determined effort, and upset that she was impatient. At that second, after being mindful of the entire scenario, I felt I didn't belong. Something had happened that dramatically changed within me like an inner shift of some kind after the near drowning.

"What I know now is, NDE experiencers don't want to be here. This sort of occurrence is extremely profound; you want to go back to your true home and know that at some point, when this lifetime completes, your family and angel-guides will come for you."

"Sign me up now!" Randy laughingly replied.

Smiling, I continued, "NDEs become more sensitive to everything around them, so living on such a difficult planet can be very challenging. Intuition is heightened and fine-tuned. NDEs begin perceiving and reviewing their lives differently. Most, if not all, want to assist in helping the world in some way."

"I'm intrigued! So, why did you really come back, Cin?" Randy inquisitively asked.

"Everything that has occurred in my life had to happen—from birth up to this point. Even my marriage and divorce were planned. My children had to be born to me and Lance. Now, I feel I'm here to help abandoned and orphaned children. I don't know more than that, unfortunately."

"Quite an honorable task ahead," Randy added.

"I don't see it as honorable. I see it as part of my contribution to humanity. Children are humankind's future. Systems, such as the foster care programs and orphanages, as they are set up now, are not working like they should. If each human takes responsibility for whatever our world needs—and there are plenty of needs out there—it doesn't have to be a giant endeavor. Our world would transform quickly. Sadly enough, most of mainstream are too enthralled with things that don't truly matter."

I could have continued talking about my near-death experience all evening, but Randy was losing interest, and I didn't want to push him too much in one night.

"Not one word was ever mentioned in my family after that destined day, but when I walked the shoreline after that, I was very curious why I felt so different. Surprisingly, I wasn't fearful of the ocean because of my childhood ordeal. I'm deeply respectful and thankful for its presence in my life. I honor the ocean's mighty strength and feel privileged that I'm close enough to this magnificent and special place where I could effortlessly go and just be. It's a safe place for me, Randy. It's my very own sanctuary when I'm down and need a calming ear or a lift of inspiration—the sea shore graciously provides without asking anything of me. I've walked the edge, where the water meets the sand, hundreds of times since then and always leave feeling at peace. Maybe those of us who've almost lost our lives, in the depths of the ocean, were spiritually initiated. And, just maybe the initiation had to take place at sea. I wonder how many near drownings there are, especially children. The ocean has more mysteries than we know. And possibly NDEs are necessary to advance humanity seeing that most come back wanting to help the world."

"Initiation? I'm intrigued, Cin." Randy's interest renewed, so I continued talking.

"I question whether I'm the only one that feels this way about initiation." Water has been used for centuries in ceremonies. Humans are mostly water, and water is vital for all life forms. It's been a source of healing and ancient divination, and it has been incorporated in religious traditions to purify. There's a mystical belief about water. A friend recently brought up that scientists from Russia discovered that water's structure is much like a nervous system—something like four hundred thousand memory cells that are information panels and have an interaction with its environment. And remembering back, Dr. Emoto's most famous experiment with water, the effects words had on it, opened my eyes. Have you seen his work?"

"Yes, pretty startling. When I first read about Dr. Emoto's work, it was difficult to comprehend. Who knew emotions and words could affect water? But it took another study years later to truly understand the importance. My son created a science experiment using two plants. One he nurtured, touched, and talked niceties. The other, he abused—screamed, yelled negative words. The results were staggering." Randy said.

"Yes, I've heard about this experiment. Plants, animals, even humans have been mistreated for too long. Much of society has lost the connection to nature that our ancestors had."

"Isn't that the truth… Sorry, Cin. Please continue."

"There's also a theory about the salt in sea water, Randy. Alchemists have called salt the fifth element. It's been stated that it has the qualities of ether, which make up heaven. Sea salt specifically has healing properties as well. We all need salt in our bodies to function. And not table salt. Table salt has no known benefits. There's so much more we have to learn about the ocean and its mysteries. I find it compelling that the first organisms didn't develop on land. They formed from beneath the depths of water. If water has this powerful, incredible memory component to it, recording and storing within its structure, maybe this was a necessary step in the evolution of humankind. Will water play a supporting role from some of the destruction going on in our world?

"Just the other day, I listened to a guy's interview about this substance found in Arizona called Ormus. Ormus is made up of various elements that have healing properties, they say. What was so compelling, is that the man interviewed said that Ormus is abundant on the ocean floor. It rises to the surface, out of the water, to the sky, to fill the clouds with this substance and falls back down to the earth. Some call this substance an *alchemical wonder*. I don't know much about Ormus, but I want to learn more."

"Cin, Cin." Randy wanted me to stop.

"Yes."

"You slipped, fell, and got swept away. I get the NDE part, and I was somewhat fascinated by the initiation piece, but now you're on this tangent?"

"A tangent? Seriously? I'm just curious. That's all!" I answered, unprepared by Randy's remark.

Randy withdrew from the conversation.

"Can I just mention one other thing?" I asked carefully.

Randy sat there looking perplexed. Trying to guess what else could possibly come out of my mouth.

"A friend was talking to a man whose wife is a marine biologist in Santa Cruz. The man stated that his wife mentioned that the ocean is going to take care of all the pollution and will get back to its natural state. I wondered, *How is that possible? Could it be Ormus?*"

Randy half smiled.

I changed the subject thinking Randy might feel I was off my rocker. "Randy, consider this. What if my family didn't make it to the beach that day? My NDE might have never happened. This was a planned occurrence, I believe. Just like most things in our lives. Lia and everyone involved had to be a part of this designed plan. What Lia experienced that day wasn't what I was learning and vice versa."

"It's sure a wild story." Randy shook his head in disbelief.

I stopped and thought of Gertie. "Think about Gertie and how that story unfolded. Explain that."

"I can't explain it. Yes, it was pretty strange," replied Randy.

"The initiation part is just a curiosity I've had. There may be nothing to it. I honestly haven't thought further about this off-the-wall feeling I've had, but I would be willing to seek out others who have had a near-drowning experience—especially in childhood—and ask them these compelling questions."

I paused. "Not too long ago, I was telling a friend about my NDE story, and he asked the most curious question. 'Cynthia, have you ever explored the fact that the giant man that rescued you was one of your guardian angels?'

"I had never thought of it, but yes, I feel one of my angels saved my life, for reasons that are beginning to make sense now. I wished I could have seen him as clearly as Lia."

"It's riveting that your eyes were caked with sand, but you could see the entire experience in heaven."

"Remarkably, I could see clearly in heaven, in full spectrum, but barely saw anything once I was rescued. Years later, I heard a story of a blind woman who had an NDE. She recounted everything, from colors to shapes and other things that she couldn't possibly know. We don't actually see with our eyes alone. We are spiritual beings, Randy. Our spirit has advanced sensory perception."

"You are full of stories!"

"Yes, it seems so, doesn't it?"

13: Finding Strength in Difficult Times

At 4:00 a.m., in haste, I sat up in bed. I had a super strange feeling. In the doorway of Randy's bedroom was the well-groomed man who was standing in the corner of the marbled room during my NDE. I gasped, turned, and shook Randy.

"What…what?" Randy opened his eyes.

"That man. That man. He's here. In the doorway."

Randy sat up half asleep. "Whattt mannn?"

"The man who was quietly observing me in heaven."

"But I don't see anyone. Are you sure you weren't dreaming?"

"No, I'm sure. I was sound asleep but sensed someone was watching. I sat up and there he was," I said in a bewildered voice.

Randy got up, checked the hallway and other rooms, then returned empty handed.

"There's no one here." He bent over to hunt for the stranger under the bed. "Not even under the bed."

We both laughed and decided to get up since we were both wide awake. It was almost the crack of dawn. We dressed and drove to the East Bay Hills of Oakland. We got out of the car and walked up a hillside to view the sun rising. Randy took me in his arms once again; we danced, and he sang a sweet love song. It was a nice feeling to settle into this romantic life. I felt safe. I felt loved and adored.

As we were driving back, Randy asked about Jonathan's accident.

"Do you truthfully want to hear this? I'm always sharing my stories. I'd like to hear a few of yours."

"In time, Cynthia Long, in time."

Hmmm...

"Well, where do I begin?" I took a big breath to help me reach back in memory to that distressful day.

"It was an early summer morning. Our family had just finished breakfast. Jon always wanted to be outside, exploring. He was an extremely active child. He jumped off the bar stool and ran out to play. I was doing the dishes when our young delivery driver frantically ran up the deck to the front door with Jonathan in his arms five minutes later. I was confused and ran to the door. The young man handed Jon to me, and all I could hear were low-toned moans coming from my three-and-a-half-year-old child. I knew something was awfully wrong and hurried to our bedroom. Lance heard the commotion and followed. I carefully placed Jon on the bed and opened his diaper. It was horrible, and I don't want to go into much of it. We rushed to the hospital. Jonathan was split open down below. He had a terrible head injury and his hip was twisted horribly. But before I into the entire story, the physician at the hospital thought I abused my son. It was beyond belief as I was dealing with more than I could possibly handle as it was!

"I was interrogated for four days of Jon's ordeal, which was the worst for him as he was critically injured. It was imperative that he had my complete attention more than ever. I tried to contact the young driver who ran over our son, but he was nowhere to be found. He ran scared. The physician and his nurse thought I was lying. I called Lance and disturbingly explained the horror, but he was drowning in his own pain, which took years to understand. I had no support. I had to deal with it alone."

"Are you kidding?"

"No, it was like a double nightmare! Finally, the fourth day, the driver squeamishly turned up and confronted the doctor with his story. I was so young, bruised to the bone. The only fight I had in me had been for my precious son."

I stopped to catch my breath and continued with my story, "I called my mother and she drove two hours to be by my side. This was a miracle in itself. She never drove by herself anywhere, let alone two hours over hills and mountains. Mom didn't even go to the store alone for many years. I was grateful and appreciated her support since I was alone and in a fearful state. We held vigil during the roughest nights. Lance's mother had our other two children, Allsia and Michael; they were only seven and five. That experience brought me back to God. I had been far removed before the accident."

I was getting very emotional, and I could tell my story was undoubtedly getting through to Randy.

"Jonathan began healing, but then contracted staph infection from a nurse that cleaned his wound daily. I caught her on a couple of occasions without gloves but had no idea Jon would be harmed by this inconsiderate act. It was another nightmare to experience. They thought Jon had meningitis, which required a spinal tap test. I couldn't cope. Lance finally stood up to be with him during another disturbing situation our son endured. His fever ran off the thermometer chart. He moaned and cried endlessly. I felt helpless. I wanted to move him to Bay Area Children's Hospital since he wasn't receiving the best of care. I was angry, but I had opposition from Lance and his family who didn't want to talk or deal with it. It was the very first incident I spoke up, but it didn't matter.

"I took the night shifts by his side. Lance's mother took the day shift. Jon was never alone. Lance's mom brought our other two children to the window outside Jonathan's room to visit at least once a week. It broke my heart to see their faces. They were frightened for their brother, and so was I. We finally brought Jon home, and he had to learn to walk again. It didn't take long for him to get back to normal."

"I've heard stories like this, and it's unimaginable how people get the strength to endure. How did you gain the strength to carry on, Cin?"

"I don't actually know. It was all a blur. Jon was facing yet another hospital visit two months later for a major kidney operation and I had to continue on. It was another difficult period since I had to deal with this mostly by myself again. Lance could never handle any sort of uneasiness or tragic event, so discussions were off limits. Jon's surgery took place and, being that it was the busy season on the family ranch, Lance chose to work. Our child could have died. Two hours out of this one day to be with me and our young son, was not too much to ask. Lance's mom was there for the surgery and very supportive, which helped ease my fears. I held that disappointment inside for many years along with other incidents, but now I have finally come to the realization that Lance didn't have the tools or a desire to learn or grow past his comfort zone.

"Anyway, Jon was in a four-bed hospital room. One child died of a heart attack the first night. She was only twelve. And another six-year-old, a sweet boy who was dying of cancer, with no one present to support him. The fourth child had his organs twisted at birth and was in for his twentieth operation. His mother and I took turns comforting the six-year-old very ill child who was all alone."

"Where on earth were his parents?" Randy disturbingly inquired.

"I was told they were young, lived far away. I do not know all of the details, but as a young mother, I could not understand. It bothered me for many years. The other mother and I sat with him daily, held his hand, and caressed his head. Tumors were growing outside of his body. He was in excruciating pain. It was difficult to keep my strength. There were so many ill children in the hospital. I became numb to cope. The brain tumors were the worst for me to withstand. It opened my eyes, my heart, and again, I was on my knees asking for God's help. When people are feeling down in their lives, they should go to a children's hospital and try to grasp what is genuinely important."

"How did you do all of that alone?" Randy asked.

"My mother-in-law was a great help. I guess God gave me the extra strength. Jonathan's surgery went well. He went home and recovered. The best part was that he remembers little. It took me awhile as I fell apart a few years later with PTSD. They had no name for it back then, but after researching, that is what I ended up with. I worked on this disorder and led through it with God's and my angel's help."

"Sorry, Cin. Wow, unbelievable!"

"Yes, it's humbling."

Randy took my hand and squeezed it.

"You are some lady. You will never face anything alone again."

He had my attention. Somehow I believed him.

14: A Past Life Connection

I wanted to talk to Randy about my friend whose home burned down. There were new developments, so I broached the subject one night after dinner. I wanted his opinion and went into the story of how my friend's husband was fired from his job. As I spoke, I noticed how Randy was now far removed and not listening. He was distracted. I asked if he was okay since the tone of his voiced had changed. I couldn't figure out what was going on; this had never happened before. He insisted that he was fine, but he was always so attentive. I was confused with the mixed messages. Perhaps he was teetering on the edge of divulging a possible issue. I finally dropped the subject and moved on. The weekend ended.

I decided to move to San Ramon to be closer to Randy. Traveling back and forth had gotten old. The move was a family affair. All three of my adult children pitched in. Randy did not offer until the last minute. I thought that was unusual, but he'd moved enough in his life, as well as helped others, that he could have been tired from even hearing the word *move*. On the day of the move we went to my large storage unit, which held all my business and personal items. As he slid the door open, he looked around at how much work there would be and said, "I'm leaving!" We all laughed knowing it was a daunting task ahead of us. It was a huge move, which took two full days. My daughter assisted beyond the call of duty. I moved two miles up the hill from Randy, which was more convenient.

Days went into weeks and we were involved with family events and parties. We went away for weekends. We danced and he sang love songs. I continued to receive greeting cards and flowers. I was a greeting-card junkie too. I was truly falling for this guy!

The next day, I called Margaret, my good friend that I had met in Brazil. I first met Margaret when I was walking toward the dining area for dinner at my posada. I noticed radiant sparkles all around her. It was a unique observation. I questioned my sanity at that moment, but the glimmer was present continuously. I thought about the intensity of Abadiania and how the uncommon area brought out the best and worse in people. For sure Margaret's attributes were illuminated! I knew she was very special and would become my spiritual godmother.

"Hi, Margaret. It's been awhile, so sorry. I've been busy. I'm in a new relationship and I just moved. How are you and your hubby?" I asked.

"Darling, we are well, thank you. It's wonderful to hear from you! A new relationship *and* a move? You have been busy! Things are good for you?"

"Yes, so far, so good."

"Lovely."

"Margaret, I must share some co-occurrences with you." I began the story of the dating site and e-mail from Randy. Then the "23 stories" and St. Joseph's church, the song my father sang when I was a child—the same song Randy's father sang to him and the odd plantation dream.

"My, oh my! This feels like a past life connection, dear! Randy sounds very charming! There's more to unfold. I'm quite sure of it! Let it play out!"

"Yes, Randy is an incredible man. Very kind, generous, and very funny!"

15: The Embarrassing Blue Face and Mrs. Walsh's Funeral

The next week was one that was necessary to lay low. I scheduled a chemical peel; my skin was fairly sun damaged due to all of the California beach years. Now, I'm paying the price. The peel was the most horrible experience I've ever had. I begged the doctor to stop applying the blue peel after almost thirty minutes—I couldn't take the extreme burning sensation any longer. I was informed that my face would be a blue tone for about a week. Jon was in the waiting room to take me home. As I walked out, he laughed.

"Mom, I didn't think your face would be this blue!" Jon snickered.

"I mentioned it a few weeks ago, Jon. I'm going to lay low for a week, thank goodness."

Jonathan smirked, and we walked to the car.

When I returned home, a phone message was waiting from Randy. He sounded very upset. I called right back, only to find out that his mother had died of a heart attack in her parked car. I felt compassion for Randy and tried to comfort him. He communicated that the rosary was in three days.

I was dead silent. *Three days? My face is blue for a week.* I muttered to myself. I didn't bring up the dilemma and just let him talk out what he needed to say.

As soon as I ended the call, I hurried to the bathroom to observe my razzle-dazzle, blue face. A horrible sight!

I didn't know what to do, so I began dialing Jen's number.

"Jen, another strange day in paradise! Mrs. Walsh just died and the rosary is in three days! I just had the blue peel, and now I look like a Smurf! Oh my gosh! What to do?"

"You know you gotta go! Jeez, nice timing!" Jen responded laughing!

"Go? Like this? I look like a Smurf. All of Randy's college friends, family…oh my God, I got to see if I can peel or at least wash some of this off."

"Good luck," Jen was belly laughing.

We hung up, and I wasn't happy…not happy at all.

For two days I tried to get my face to look half human with no luck. Randy stopped by and confirmed my Smurf look and was holding his humor, mostly because he was in mourning and partly because he was considerate. By the third day, it was a bit better but not enough to be out in the public eye. Mrs. Walsh's rosary happened quickly. I tested different approaches. Different hats and sunglasses. I tried to roughly wash more of the neon blue off but only with minimal luck. My face hurt, and I was very raw and almost bleeding in different spots. I cried while looking at myself in the mirror. Finally, I came to the realization that I had to "woman up" and remember that the most important part was to be there for Randy.

On the eve of the rosary, I sat with my hat and glasses in the very back of the mortuary. Different people walked up and asked what was going on with my blue look. Most smiled, some chuckled, but I handled it. Randy was appreciative and so was his family. The funeral the next day was lovely. Randy was the spokesperson during the service.

I learned more history of the Walsh family as Randy reminisced with the guests at the church. Mrs. Walsh certainly had a very challenging life for many years, raising eight children on her own. It was a giant feat, and she could now look upon her life with amazement!

16: Spirits, Mexico, and the Red Gown's Royal Entrance

That night, I woke up sensing two spirit-like beings at my bedroom door. I sat up and waited. I felt these beings pause for some reason. They then magically emerged through the closed door. It was Mrs. Walsh and her deceased sister. The sister was coaching Mrs. Walsh; it was as if she was confused with this new way to enter a room. How did I know this? It's a bit challenging to explain, but I just had an understanding. Mrs. Walsh began communicating that she wanted her children to spend time in her home before, during, and after the services. This was very important to her. Her ultimate wish: for her children to begin to get along. Then, poof! Gone! I blessed her way, and I expressed to Randy the importance of this communication the next morning. He relayed the message to his siblings.

One November morning, Randy called and asked if I wanted to go to Mexico for my birthday the following month. He mentioned that his family had a condo there. I'm a traveler and open to any adventure. The trip went as planned and in no time we were on an airplane to Cabo San Lucas where we rented a car and drove to his family's timeshare condo. As we pulled in, some of the units were being worked on, and the noise from all the machinery was not appealing. Randy went to the main lobby to ask about the construction. He was told it would go on daily for another few weeks. He was not happy. Plan B came into effect. We found a hotel right on the beach.

The next day we went to see the famous Hotel California, which took us a good four hours to drive the winding roads. We walked around the small village enjoying the atmosphere and the local artists' works. We ended up eating lunch across the street from the famous hotel while listening to piped-in music as it bellowed from the outside entrance. The restaurant had thousands upon thousands of names, inside and out-side, of the travelers who ventured to it. We wanted to place our names somewhere outside, but the waiter informed us that there was very little room left.

Only one name would fit on one side and the other name on the opposite side. *For real?* I didn't like the idea and felt uncomfortable, but we ended up writing our names far removed from the others. The waiter showed up and noticed our names and informed us that they would paint over it since that area was off limits. I found it curious and didn't realize that they would paint over the names.

"It's like we were never here! I wonder what that means." I grumbled to Randy. He had no response.

We meandered back to our hotel in Cabo after our meal. I wasn't looking forward to the long winding drive. I got motion sickness and Randy graciously searched for a place where I could get something salty to settle my stomach. After much effort, we found a far-removed, dated store and questioned if he would find anything useful. Randy walked out with his hands full of salted-bagged items. A half bag of chips relieved my nausea just when we arrived at the hotel. We took our showers and prepared to go to dinner.

It was dusk. Randy and I wandered through a small area in the village toward an Italian restaurant that was recommended. As we strolled toward the restaurant, we were distracted by a large picture win-dow displaying a gorgeous, red silk formal gown. We nonchalantly glanced at one another and smiled. I knew he was ruminating over purchasing it, but we both remained quiet as we immediately entered the alcove of the restaurant. The hostess seated us outside in the inviting garden area. It was a warm, comfortable evening. As we finished our lovely dinner, Randy kindly conveyed, "Cin, I want to buy that gown for you. It was made just for you!"

"I had a feeling that was on your mind! But *no*, I cannot accept the offer!" I candidly replied.

"Please, Cin, let's at least see if it fits you."

I wasn't so sure I could convince Randy not to purchase it. Where would I wear a gown like that? We reside in California. I mostly lived an informal life. It just didn't make sense.

We briskly walked to the shop, but it was closed. Randy was insistent and on a mission to go back for the gown. The following day, as we entered the boutique, there was a smiling sixty-year-old woman who gave us the impression she was in charge.

"Hello, is it possible for my girlfriend to try on the gown in the window?" Randy asked.

The woman acted perplexed. "*No comprende!*" Other Spanish words were pouring out, but that was all we could understand. She quickly scurried to the back room only to return with a younger woman who spoke English pretty well. Randy asked again. In silence, the younger woman took the silk formal off the mannequin and handed me the gown. She pointed to an antique room divider set up in the corner for changing. I slipped this beautiful work of art on. It didn't fit. I thought that was a good sign for Randy not to spend his money! I called out to Randy to inform him. He asked the younger woman if it could be altered. The elder woman walked behind the divider, "*Si.*" That was it—he purchased the beautiful red silk gown for me on the spot! We picked it up the following day.

I felt very special and touched by Randy's generosity but wondered if the gown would just sit in the closet collecting dust.

At the hotel that night around midnight, we began hearing loud instrumental Latin music. We tossed and turned until 3:00 a.m. Randy had enough at that point and was going down to where the foreign sound was coming from to ask them to keep it down. I decided to go with him, and we followed the beat of the music to the party. Next to the ocean, there was a large, white tent with torches lining the perimeter, and an easel with a framed photo and words in Spanish. The number forty was next to the words. We assumed it was the recipient's fortieth birthday since most of the people were of that age group. Randy and I tried to get the attention of a few people, but without success. We finally found someone who spoke English and he acted sympathetic but disappeared into the party. We walked back to our room and tried to sleep, but it was just more tossing and turning.

By 5:00 a.m. the music stopped. Randy was very upset and was determined to talk to management. A few hours later he almost sprinted down to the front desk. I followed behind. Randy asked for the manager as he approached the front desk. His complaint fell upon deaf ears. Apparently, the hotel was frequently paid well to host private parties. Nothing Randy expressed mattered. I noticed Randy's Irish face getting red. He began pointing his finger and then raising his voice. I stepped back, then turned and walked away. Randy was also an all-star boxer in college, and I thought perhaps he would reach over and pull the guy from behind the counter and punch him. I wanted that thought to go away immediately!

135

I nervously proceeded back towards Randy. I took his arm and drew him towards me to whisper, "Let this go! It's no use." Randy was so wound up and not listening! It brought back some uncomfortable memories. My own Irish father had a temper like that and it took years to heal from it. Finally, he gave up and we walked away. I thought to myself, *Should I start another mental notebook?* The note I was taking now was not a favorable one.

I eventually forgot about that incident in Mexico and gave Randy the benefit of doubt considering he was exhausted and had a legitimate gripe.

* * *

I was after Randy for awhile to drive up to San Francisco to visit St. Joseph's. He hadn't been there in years, and I was overdue for a visit. We made plans and drove up to the city on Saturday. As we entered the church, there was a small wedding in progress. We found a seat in the middle of the church; the wedding was small and intimate. We sat there observing the special day.

Randy leaned over. "Cin, this could be us. Would you want to marry here?"

I hesitantly paused. "Marry? Hmmm, possibly."

I wasn't sure why I had pulled thoughts. I held his hand while the vows were spoken.

After, we walked around and spent some time at St. Joseph's shrine and Our Lady's. We whispered our prayers as we knelt. I meditated for a bit. We completed our ritual and went to dinner. The day was perfect like most days of our new life.

One day, I was mulling over the idea of a date night. I mentioned it to Randy during one of our many daily conversations. He loved the idea. We made a plan for the next Saturday night.

I prepared a special meal that Randy was fond of. The whole nine yards, which included wearing the beautiful red silk gown he had bought for me in Mexico. I purchased a tiara and a wand to set the stage. I worked all day to make it perfect. Early that evening, the doorbell rang. I opened the front door; Randy stood there, with flowers in hand. He was in awe that I was wearing the lovely gown he had purchased. He leaned over and kissed me in his sweet manner.

"Cin, you look beautiful!"

"Thank you! How do you like the tiara and wand?"

"The wand?" Randy jokingly said, "I have a good idea for the wand later!"

We both laughed out loud.

I went into the kitchen and prepared his favorite drink. I poured my usual, chardonnay. I cranked up the music. We danced fast, then slow, and finally hugged.

"Cin, you made this night very special. Everything is perfect. You are the best."

"Randy, you are always treating me like a queen. I want to also show you how special you are."

He smiled and we sat to eat our meal—candles ablaze, with my right hand lightly embracing his left. This was a comforting habit of ours. We danced again after dinner, leaving the dishes. We aimed straight to the bedroom, slowly seducing… It was a great date night!

17: Two-Toned Shoes Manifested, Past Lives, and Karma

After I moved to San Ramon, we spent more time at my home since I felt more comfortable there. But every so often, I would do Randy's laundry or his bedroom would need some attention—clothes folded, hung up, and organizing of the general area. I was over one day straightening up. I went into his closet and hung some shirts in the corner. I glanced down and noticed a pair of shoes tucked far back in the closet. I bent down and pulled them out. Two-toned shoes! Randy had the exact two-toned shoes that were in my dream. I got a chill and thought, *What in the world?*

I paused and gathered the details of the Plantation dream from memory while I was hanging up the rest of his clothes. My new mental notebook earned two entries.

We began spending some time with my mom. The very first visit when Randy and my mother met, it was like they knew each other. It was the oddest situation. They would look at each other with fondness in their eyes as though they were old friends. On occasion I would tell him, "You and my mother should be the ones dating."

He would chuckle and discount my statement. I was sure there was more to come to light, but I couldn't put it together just yet. Randy would cater to my mother, and she would eat it up. One day we were at her home in San Jose for a visit. My mom pulled out some old photographs, and we were sorting through them. I was pointing to photos of relatives and reminiscing about some family history with Randy. Even though my parents divorced years ago and my father passed away, my mother still had traces of my father in her life, including photos. I was flipping through an old, torn album I had never seen before when I happened upon a photo of an old man who strikingly resembled my father in my plantation dream.

"Who is this, Mom?"

"It's your great, great grandfather. Look on the back. It should say."

I turned to the back and read "Samuel Barton Long—Savannah, Georgia." I was stopped dead in my tracks. I disturbingly turned the album page and changed the subject. The synchronicities were beginning to frighten me.

How could this be true? Was I reliving a past life? I began putting two and two together. I felt that my mother was my sister in that dream. I found that to be peculiar. My mother and I had been at odds with one another for years. Could this be validation? Past life, unfinished business? Did I hurt my mother, when she was possibly my sister? Was Randy, William? How about those two-toned shoes William wore in the dream that I found in Randy's closet?

I couldn't wait to speak to my godmother, Margaret, about what had unfolded. I was thoroughly confused and flustered. We finished up in San Jose and drove home. I held this latest revelation close since it was beyond odd.

The next day, I kept looking at the clock for a perfect moment to call Margaret. The time difference made it such that I had to catch her before she turned off her phone.

"Hi, Margaret," I sighed in relief when she answered. "How are you and your hubby? It's been awhile since we spoke. My new relationship is taking lots of my time and energy!"

"Hi, Cindy. Good to hear from you. Yes, I can imagine. We are doing well. We may move closer to my daughter since I'm going to be traveling and need someone to watch our home. We live in a remote area and a bit too far for family to drive."

"Well, Margaret, your home is large, and it's becoming a big chore for you and Gerald."

"Yes."

"I have a weird situation that has come up, Margaret. Please give me your take on it."

I went into the story with Margaret, and this was her response, "Cynthia, I sense you are clearing karma with your mother in this lifetime. Your mother definitely was your sister in the dream. I also sense Randy was William. And it feels like you were in the middle of their breakup in the past life in Georgia? Do you recall?"

"I don't recall since the dream ended at the lake, but it surely feels this way, Margaret! My mother and I have had many issues through the years. Partly because of my father and my close relationship with him, but does a past life have a role also?" I responded in a cautious manner, blown away by the entire scenario and yearning for Margaret's wisdom.

"Margaret, you cannot imagine how my mother and Randy connected. It's surely as if they knew one another before. I've told Randy every now and again that he should date my mother since their bond is so uncanny."

"Fascinating! Well, we are in times now to clear all karma! We incarnate in soul groups, as you well know. So, you have had lives with different family members, friends, and lovers. You have karma with Randy as well."

"Karma with Randy? Is it good karma?" I was puzzled.

Margaret wavered almost like she wanted to word this delicately. "You have unfinished business with Randy. He will hand you a gift later on, but you will not see it at first."

"Unfinished business? What do you mean?"

"You have had some very magnetic synchronicities with him, yes?"

"Yes, Margaret. The synchronicities are piling up! First, him finding me, like a needle in a haystack, and then St. Joseph's Church. Can you believe it was rebuilt in 1923 and by his grandfather? The list goes on, but the latest, Margaret, is disturbing. And get this...I just found the same two-toned shoes that William was wearing in my dream, in Randy's closet!"

"Astonishing!" Margaret sounded jolted. There was a lull. "First, all the synchronicities sound like you are in a fated relationship. And the two-toned shoes—my, oh my. Let it play out, dear."

"Let it play out? I'm beginning to feel uneasy, Margaret."

"Yes, let it play out. You will be fine. Don't worry. Darling, I need to run. We'll talk in a week or so. Love you..."

"Love you too, Margaret... Oh, Margaret, one last thing. What sort of gift will Randy hand me?"

"Sweetheart, just go with the flow for now. It will all make sense moving forward. Bye. Love you!"

"Love you, Margaret…"

I hung up, perplexed.

18: Sign Posts

The next week, Randy was out of town on business. I was winding down for the evening when I got an unexpected, disconcerting feeling. I kept hearing, *Go to your computer and check the dating website where Randy found you, and type in his user name.*

Is my mind playing tricks on me? Am I getting suspicious after the conversation with Margaret? I felt like I was being pushed out of bed. I kept saying, "This is nuts! What in the world am I doing?"

I sat at the computer for at least five minutes contemplating, ready to type, but my fingers lay frozen on the keypad. There were no clues that Randy would be doing anything out of integrity. I trusted him, and he trusted me. Suddenly, I got another push. *Jeez.* My feelings grew very strong, and so I went with what I felt. I got onto the dating site and typed Randy's user name.

There, before my eyes, was Randy's profile…my heart sank! I stiffened with disbelief. I began getting dizzy and left the computer room. I held my chest and cried.

What's going on? I reviewed our relationship. Nothing showed up odd, or if it did, I wasn't noticing. I went back to the computer and back to the site. I typed in his user name again. I now noticed he was online chatting. *Hmmm… Chatting, with whom?*

I couldn't breathe. I closed my eyes and reopened them like it was a bad dream. I wanted this to go away. I decided to copy the page, and e-mail it to Randy. After sending it, the phone rang two minutes later. Two minutes? I answered, and it was Randy.

"Cin, Cin?"

I had no breath to speak to him. I hung up. He called back. I hung up again! He called once more. I let it ring and ring. He left a message.

I eyed my phone wondering if I should listen to the message or just wait until I felt better. I turned it off and settled down for an hour to get my bearings. After an hour, I reached for my cell phone and typed in my passcode. One new message.

"Cin, I need to talk to you. You are taking this the wrong way. I was talking to a friend I hadn't communicated with in awhile. She mentioned she wanted to get on this dating site but needed assistance. I told her I had my profile on hold since I was in a relationship, but I could bring it up and she could see what I wrote. On this dating site you can now correspond via instant messaging. I would never do anything to hurt you, ever! Please call me back. I am beside myself!"

I put down my phone and just watched it as it began ringing off the hook again. I sank into bed and put the covers over my head. *This is just a bad dream!*

The next day, Randy flew in from his business trip and aimed straight for my home. The doorbell rang and I froze. I honestly didn't want to answer the door. I was devastated and wanted to just hide. I then thought, *This isn't right.* It was urgent to talk about this bizarre situation. I opened the door after five bell rings. He and I just stared at each other.

"Cin, I didn't sleep a wink all night."

"I didn't either."

Randy whisked in and proceeded to the living room.

We talked for a few hours and things smoothed over. Maybe I was looking into this too much after what Margaret had mentioned.

Randy and I embraced, and he left.

I called Jen and mentioned what had occurred. She said, "We will see what happens next. It sounds like he's telling the truth."

"Jen, I just don't know what to surmise."

"Just pay attention and see what comes about. I gotta go. Chat later."

"Okay, thank you. Goodbye."

I went into the living area of my home to settle down and meditate. Meditation had previously been part of my life, but I had recently been ignoring it. I prayed and then sat for at least a half hour. It was just what I deserved. I felt a sense of peace that had been misplaced. I began reminiscing again about my journey to Brazil.

* * *

I was walking down the dusty dirt road to The Casa to meet up with the tour guide and my friend Sal. We filed into a synchronized configuration with dozens of others dressed in white attire. As I entered the black iron gates to the blue-trimmed, white-washed center, it was filled with people in white as well. I asked a few, who behaved like volunteers, if they spoke English. One man pointed to another not far from where I was standing. I approached him.

"Hello, so you speak English?"

"Yes."

"This is my first visit here, and I would like to know what to do."

The man took me to the main area of the center and explained the procedure. I thanked him and took a seat.

While taking in the humble setting, I noticed a slightly elevated stage area surrounded by at least a hundred people closely sitting together on old metal chairs. I took a quick look around, searching for the tour guide and Sal. A man climbed the two stairs to the podium that was situated on the raised wooden-built stage and started speaking in Portuguese.

"Great. I have no idea what he's saying," I mumbled out loud.

He pointed to a blue door that led somewhere.

Most everyone understood and abruptly stood and hastily formed two lines. I sat there totally confused about which line to get into. I remembered that the man mentioned there's a line for first timers and then a line for those who had a healing and needed further instructions from John of God.

I continued my search around the crowded space and noticed my guide. I got up excitedly and ask her what to do. She again explained the procedure. The first and second rooms were set up for meditation. John of God was located in the third room. In the fourth area, one would sit and pray with the group leaders and then be led outside for a meal.

I started for the end of the first very long line and waited. It began to move slowly. Finally, I entered the first room as instructed. I noticed rows and rows of meditators in white to my left. I began feeling different. I don't know how to explain it since I've never felt this way before.

I inched closer to the second room. This room was also filled with people meditating. The area was used to continue cleansing the individual, according to those I listened to later. All of a sudden, as I stood there in line, a small number of people began falling off their chairs. I was beyond startled. It was as though they had died. I was now wondering if I should not be here. I quickly scanned the crowded room. Not one person meditating got up to help. Was I seeing something that didn't happen? I wanted to leave, but I couldn't move. I caught the eyes of a few who were in line. I felt they were also almost in a panic state, which assured me that this was for real. All of a sudden I heard rustling from behind. There was a small group of people trailing up to the individuals lying on the floor. They were tapped upon and spoken to. The individuals awoke and were helped up and brought to the infirmary. This eased my concerns and those around me. I refocused on the line ahead as it moved forward. I noticed there were only six more people ahead of me.

I asked God for help to relax. This entire scene was pretty bizarre, and I didn't know what to think or how to assess what just took place.

Finally, it was my turn. I slowly and carefully walked up to John of God. He appeared to be scanning my body, spoke a little Portuguese, and pointed to the second meditation room. I looked around for assistance since I wasn't sure what to do. Someone stepped forward and mentioned that I must meditate twice a day, every day for healing to occur. For now, I was to meditate in the second room. I spotted Sal and took a seat near him.

The following morning Sal and I entered the main hall of The Casa and sat down. I began feeling dizzy. I mentioned this peculiar sensation to Sal. We got up after the morning instructions, entered the first meditation room, and ended up toward the back and took a seat. Sal and I started our meditation, but the dizziness got worse. I placed my head on the back of the wooden bench I shared with others on to see if it would subside. It was now overwhelming. I was now concerned and inched my way slowly to Sal and asked him to seek some assistance. Sal appeared worried as he had never seen me in this state and rushed from his seat to get help. Two of The Casa volunteers and Sal approached. I was helped up and ushered to the infirmary where I had witnessed others being led the day before.

As I lay on the hospital bed, one kind lady ambled close and in a low voice advised me to keep my eyes shut. I thought that was odd, but I obeyed. She made known that I had received an operation. The light headedness subsided, but abruptly I had to use the restroom—and quick. I opened my eyes a hair and scanned the room. Two assistants were sitting in the corner on alert as there were ill patients scattered around the large infirmary. I called out, and one woman got up from her seat and asked what my problem was about.

"I need to use the restroom. Can I open my eyes?"

"Yes."

As the woman pointed to a door in the corner of the room, I carefully arose and wondered if I would be okay or possibly faint and fall upon the hard floor under me. I slowly entered the restroom and pulled up my white skirt while noticing that both of the zippered compartments to my money belt were totally unzipped. "That's freaky. How did that happen?" I spouted out loud. I finished my duty and wobbled toward the bed to lie back down. The same volunteer had a watchful eye, approached, and expressed that I could leave if I didn't feel weak, but it was crucial I go back to my posada and rest for twenty-four hours. I cautiously got up and walked outside toward the soup kitchen where the volunteers—who made the soup—and everyone else gathered after

148

the session.

I stood in the lengthy soup line and began to feel woozy once again. I needed to sit. I searched for an empty spot in the crowded eating area. I asked someone in line if they could bring my soup, explaining that I had just received an operation. I finally found a seat, and my soup was delivered by the considerate person. I hoped the soup would help ease the weird feeling, but it did not subside. I hurriedly finished and warily wobbled over to summon a taxi outside the iron gates of The Casa to get back to my posada since it was clear I needed to rest.

That night I awoke to someone or something working on my body. Once I was awake, it departed. I asked about this wild feeling later on, and I was told that the spirits have the capability to work on individuals while they sleep, which I found curious. I felt better the next day and continued the four to six hours of daily meditation.

* * *

I awoke from my memory of this experience at The Casa and knew I must get back into the meditation practice.

One day I went to Randy's home to do some laundry and straighten up a bit. I always used his computer while finishing up a load of wash. I thought to kill some time and went online. I typed "A" in the browser because I wanted to go to a spiritual website that began with A. When I typed in A, the history of all the As surfaced on the drop-down menu. I scanned and look at the As that dropped down.

Anna's sexy photos. April's sex shop. I clicked on Anna's link. Nude photos. I clicked on April's sex shop, more nude photos. I then went to B. And then C, D, E, F, and so on. There were a few dating sites. I was distressed once again!

19: Trust

"What the hell is going on?" I called Jen on my cell phone and brought up what I found.

Jen responded, "Paul goes to porn sites too. This is what some guys do."

I listened, but wasn't convinced. "There were some dating sites too. Wow, Jen, I'm feeling obsessive, and this is not me!" I responded insecurely.

"Did you go to the dating sites to see if he's on there?" Jen continued to question.

"Not yet. I'll go now."

I typed Randy's screen name on a couple of dating sites that showed up on his computer—zilch.

"I'm going to go. I feel ill. I need to confront him. I don't like keeping things like this inside. Thanks, Jen."

"Keep your eyes and ears open. And keep me posted. Bye!"

Keep my eyes and ears open? Why do I need to do this? This is bullshit. I've never been through anything like this. It's like high school immaturity! I said to myself.

I left his home. It didn't feel good to stay in that environment. I wanted to be in my own cocoon. I phoned Randy and asked him to come over when he got off work; I wanted to talk to him. He was subdued for a few seconds. "Okaaay… I'll be there in a few hours."

He was in disbelief when I mentioned what I found on his computer.

"Cin, you know my brother has been staying with me while he's looking for a place to live in the area. I'm going to talk to him. I would never hurt you, Cin. You mean the world to me. I'm devastated and don't know what else to say to you…"

As I studied Randy, I was very confused. I wanted to trust him. Randy's brother was at his home a few days prior. I had to let this go as well.

20: Parallel Universe?

I was not myself for a few days. Randy was very patient. He sent flowers and a beautiful card. He eased my uncertainty in the few months following. Everything appeared perfect. We prepared a trip to Maui for a vacation. It was a welcome break!

One day while in Maui, we were talking and he changed his tone and mannerism in the conversation again. I was perplexed what that was about since it had happened one other time. His voice was different. Randy acted like I was just a person he knew, not his partner. It was disturbing. I took another mental note. This behavior passed, and we went to lay by the pool, read, and ate our lunch. Randy mentioned he had to go do an errand and left for awhile. He came back all smiles. He unexpectedly made an appointment for a spa treatment and a couples' massage.

"Cin, I made an appointment for 1:00 spa treatment for you and a 3:00 couples' massage outside in the garden area of the hotel."

I love massages and he does too. I was grateful. We had a lovely day. That night we went dancing under the moonlight after a special dinner. He took me in his arms, held me close, and began singing another love song. Suddenly I wasn't as receptive. Something had swooped over me.

The very next day Randy called down to the spa for another massage and asked for the same young lady. He was put on hold for at least ten minutes. The woman who answered the phone returned and informed him that the massage therapist felt uncomfortable and had declined to give him a massage due to the fact he had scabs and flaky skin.

He raised his voice and was now furious. Randy asked for the hotel manager. I tried to calm him down with no avail. He went rushing downstairs. I stepped back from this drama and started praying. I knew his forceful approach wouldn't work even though I felt this situation was not handled professionally by the spa. Granted, he had flaky skin, but no scabs. It was clear they needed to train their staff better, but his lashing out got me queasy once again. I was now assessing his temper for the second time and wondered if I could live with this. Eventually it all got sorted out, but now my notebook was growing in size.

The Maui vacation for the most part was relaxing. Maui is my favorite of all the islands, mostly because it was the home of my grandmother's family on my father's side.

Our life moved forward, and we were both very busy with our work. I received an e-mail about a couples' retreat in Ben Lomond and forwarded it to Randy. He immediately wrote back and expressed that if I really wanted to go, he would make a reservation. I was hopeful that just maybe we could work on our relationship. Two days later the reservation was set, but it was not until November. I was disappointed it wasn't sooner as it was urgent and we needed some assistance now.

One day Randy surprised me with a weekend getaway to Carmel. He mentioned it was also an early birthday gift. It was a welcomed mental health break, or so I thought.

The weekend arrived and we were on our way to Carmel. We dropped off our suitcases at the hotel in Carmel and bound for Monterey to Randy's favorite restaurant, the one we went to on our first date.

"Cin, let's stop at this boutique, I want to buy you an outfit. Another early birthday gift, and then I'd like to go to this bar I've been to a few times and have a drink before dinner."

"Okay."

He was insistent about the outfit part; however, I was hesitant. When we got to the boutique, he chose a few things and asked me to look around to see if anything was appealing. I tried on the chosen outfits and decided on one. We left and began driving down a very dark and winding road.

"Thank you for the birthday gift, Randy."

"You're very welcome, sweetie."

Randy had to put the bright lights on intermittently to see. All of a sudden, a deer came out of nowhere, jumping off the hill and flew in front of our car—looking at me specifically, straight in the eyes! It was a miracle we did not hit him!

While almost jumping out of my seat, I uttered, "Hmmm, deer in the headlights? This isn't a good sign!"

Randy turned ardently and gave a blank stare. I didn't know what that meant, but maybe he was on edge from the incident.

We had difficulty finding parking, so I asked Gertie for a close parking place. Randy frowned—he'd undeniably had enough of Gertie. We were coming around again when a car pulled out right in front of the bar.

I said nothing. Randy said nothing.

Randy got out of the car. I waited for him to open my door. I wondered whether the ritual had ended. Randy walked casually from his side, opened my car door, offered his hand, helped me out, and shut the door.

We found a place to sit at the bar. We had a casual conversation with the female bartender. Randy excused himself to take a call. This had been happening more and more the past few months. The female bartender peered from afar, aiming straight for my eyes, and said out of the blue, "This will be the last time you'll be with him."

"What?" I was now looking like someone had just died. This was the most bizarre thing that had just come out of nowhere. Or did it?

I wanted to ask her a few questions, but Randy returned and wanted to leave. We finished our drinks. Upon leaving, I briefly focused on the bartender who half smiled like she held a secret. I wasn't sure whether I had heard the statement correctly, so I remained silent.

Afterward, I questioned my hesitancy. I should have confronted the woman, but it was such a wild and paralyzing experience, I was taken back and didn't know what to think or do.

In silence, we drove to the restaurant by the pier. Again I waited for Randy to open my car door. Now I was beginning to look at this so-called courtesy as superficial in nature. I was still trying to recover from what the bartender had burst out.

We walked down the steep cement stairs into the seaside restaurant. I noticed the same waitress who had served us on our first date. We were seated and handed menus. Randy was in awe of a CD that was playing. He asked the waitress who the artist was. She replied, "Rod Stewart." We both were surprised it was Rod Stewart. Randy excused himself and went to the bathroom. The waitress returned like she was in this trance state and said, "You will not be dating this man too much longer."

Randy immediately walked up behind the woman, startling us both. She abruptly left the table, flustered. By this time, I was stunned. I suspected he may have brought other women to these two places. Or, was I in another reality? Miles away from the moment, the two incidents became so surreal. I didn't listen to anything Randy had to say the entire evening. We finished our meal, and before we walked up the stairs, I grabbed some matches that were sitting in a bowl by the register.

Somehow we got through the weekend. When I returned home, I was eager to call the restaurant and speak to the waitress. I searched and found the matches that ended up at the bottom of my purse and slowly dialed the number. I asked the person answering the phone if the sixty-something lady with her hair in a twist was there. I was in luck. She answered the phone in a rushed and busy manner. I explained who I was, referencing the Rod Stewart CD. She remembered Randy and I and asked if we had purchased the CD yet.

"No, not yet."

I asked what she meant when she revealed that I wouldn't be dating Randy much longer. She paused like she was stumped.

"I never said such a thing!"

So I asked again. "When my boyfriend went to the bathroom, you exclaimed that I wasn't going to be dating him much longer."

"No, that wasn't me!"

I couldn't grasp why this was happening. I thanked her for her time and hung up. I studied the clock, counting hours out loud—I needed to reach Margaret.

I shook while I dialed Margaret's number.

"Margaret, I'm so glad you answered your phone. Do you have a moment to chat? I have a lot to get off my chest. What has just occurred is way beyond anything I could even imagine!" I went into the entire scene with Margaret. I could almost feel that she knew already

156

by her wise silence.

"I was stricken by two women at two separate restaurants, who gave me eerie news. It was like they were in a trance state, Margaret, and I was in another time line."

"Darling, this is playing out the way it's supposed to. These women were warning you. Remember, anything less than truth will eventually break down. You do have some efficient angels helping!"

"Efficient angels helping? I'm wound up at this point! I cannot understand why they keep pushing me into this relationship, Margaret. I was guarded and unsure for so long. I'm actually angry with my angels right now and want to *fire them*! This has been very painful. Never in my wildest dreams did I believe this would ever happen! Not when I'm fifty-one."

"Cynthia, you are clearing karma. It's past life. You're almost there!"

"Almost there? What in the world did I do to deserve this? Damn! Margaret, I'm worn out!"

"Cynthia, I know this is difficult, but remember that earth is a learning planet, full of lessons! We don't grow much when things are perfect."

"Margaret, I'm not asking for perfect. Randy behaved perfect though. I now yearn for normal. The saying 'too good to be true' wasn't created for no reason! And guess what? I also called the waitress at the sea-side restaurant. She doesn't even remember what she had burst out about not dating Randy much longer. Am I going insane?"

"This is very intriguing. I've never heard of anything like this before. I honestly feel your angels are simply magnificent! You'll be fine. Hang in there."

"This is beyond my imagination, Margaret. It feels like I'm hanging by a thread. My angels, magnificent? Right now I need a serious pow-wow with them!"

"We'll talk in a few days. I will light a candle and pray for you. Cynthia, you must meditate to help you get through this. Bye for now. Love you…"

I couldn't imagine meditating. I was too wound up! I got off the phone and tried to focus, but everything was running together. I got into my car and drove frantically to Randy's therapist's office, which was a mile from Randy's home. I had seen her once before and hoped she would agree to see me again.

I kept repeating silently what Margaret conveyed, *Nothing less than truth will begin to break down.*

I unsteadily climbed the stairs to the therapist's office and entered the main door. She was inside and was startled when I wandered inside. Randy had been with this therapist for several years, so she, I thought, knew him well.

"Sarah, I need to speak to you. I'm about to end my relationship with Randy. Are you free to talk?"

She prudently examined my mannerisms. Sarah's facial expression conveyed she was well aware of the issues at hand. "Come in and have a seat, and tell me what's going on."

Most everything spewed out of my mouth. She appeared uncertain and chose her words carefully. It was like Sarah thought I was making it up and defended Randy to the end. I left questioning, *Am I nuts?*

This isn't happening, is it? I left beginning to sense that this entire scenario was meant to be the way it was turning out, just like Margaret said it would.

I drove home like a crazy woman. My thoughts were steering toward calling Jeff—Randy's friend, a guy I thought was my friend too. I ran in the house and searched for his number. Finally, I found it and started dialing. I began accepting that I was becoming obsessive. I hung up. I stood there eyeing the phone. Either this next communication would be the avenue to make some sense out of this nightmare or a dead end. This dysfunctional behavior got a hold of me and I dialed once more.

The phone rang and rang. Maybe this wasn't meant to be. On the last ring, Jeff picked up. I become fearful.

"Hellooo, Jeff. This is Cynthia."

"Hi, Cin, how are you?"

"Not well, Jeff." I cautiously began with just a few things, not much detail to see where Jeff was. I knew Randy confided in him about our relationship. The direction Jeff was going proved he was siding with Randy, and there was no use to continue our conversation.

The last thing Jeff said was, "What you believe could be a self-fulfilling prophecy."

We hung up and all the obsessive feelings that spewed out with Sarah and Jeff were totally gone with the wind. I was worn out.

21: Light Night of the Soul?

There were days I felt most alone. I knew I was experiencing the dark night of the soul. There was a lot of work to do on the inside of me. I was slipping and wanted to get myself back to where I used to be. I meditated and prayed, when I could settle down.

I thought about the raccoons and the message they provided. Then, our Cabo vacation, how we had a choice to split up our names or risk them being painted over. I opted for risking them being painted over. Either way, it was a clear sign.

I knew I needed to let Randy be the one to make the final move. I rarely called him. He was the one who made the effort.

One day he asked me to go with him to see his sweet aunt. I was on the fence about going but put our issues aside. I knew Aunt Lil's life was winding down and this might be my last chance. Randy picked me up and drove to the care home. We were conversing off and on. I didn't have much to say. I minded my manners and held my tongue with great difficulty, but not much longer. I was drawn to an area of the sweater he was wearing, and zoomed in to a semi-long blonde hair attached. I casually pulled it off of him as he was driving but didn't mention it.

I kept hearing, *Stand back to look in, Cynthia. Deep breaths, you will get through this.* I began reviewing the things that had occurred. I paid attention to everything now. Our visit with Aunt Lil was pleasant. I silently expressed my goodbyes.

The couples' retreat was upon us. I clearly didn't want to go. Too much had happened, but maybe this would help me personally. I was a fragile and bewildered person.

We drove up Friday afternoon. The car permeated a troubled stillness. It was clear Randy and I were on our way out of this relationship. As we climbed the mountain to Ben Lomond, it was such a tranquil setting. At least we got that. We settled into our room and walked over to the retreat center's building. There were at least fifteen couples scattered and sitting in front of the group leaders, a husband and wife team. Each participant was asked to volunteer in some way for the weekend. Randy and I were in charge of kitchen duty, the setting of dining area, and clean up. We had a crew. I sporadically forgot the issues at hand and tried to make the best of the weekend. I spent a lot of time talking to other couples. We had some fun when we were with others. We cranked the music, and Randy and I danced through the kitchen and dining area in front of the group. They were amused. The crew caught on and joined us.

I knew this would be our last dance.

We had different group therapy, role-playing sessions throughout the weekend. It was somewhat helpful. Randy and I talked about a few issues, but there was so much more to uncover. There was one session I was hesitant: each partner got up in front of the entire group and expressed what they loved about the other partner. When it was my turn, I panicked. I wanted to express to Randy and the group the wonderful and kind things he did for me, but the negative, unfinished business clouded my mind.

I was raw with the recent events that had achingly unraveled. Something came forward, and I don't even recall what it was. I couldn't say any more; I was blocked. It was if my angels placed their hands over my mouth. I sat down dismayed. Randy was clearly hurt, which brought out anger. He moved in close to my ear and badgered. The session ended and he didn't let up. I wanted to just run away. I totally lost myself and didn't have the courage or strength to stand up to him and all the issues at hand. Randy eventually got over it, like in Mexico and Maui, but this time I was the target.

I was sinking further into the depths of codependency and losing myself. The weekend ended and we drove home, mostly in silence.

I thought about my mother and her relationship with my father. I vowed I would never follow in her footsteps, but here I was a second time. I reviewed the weekend over and over and was pretty despondent when I returned home.

The next morning I needed my friends. I yearned for normal.

"Hello, Margaret. Can you chat?"

"Yes, darling. How are you?"

"How am I?" I restlessly voiced what unfolded the last weekend at the couples' retreat. "Margaret, I want to get what I know out in the open with Randy and move on. I'm lost in a stormy sea and sinking. I must end this for my sanity." I started to sob.

"I have a feeling it's coming to an end fairly soon. Please let him do the breakup," Margaret stressed.

"Margaret, I was in a few puzzling incidents in the past with Randy where he changed his voice and mannerisms, and he didn't even act like I was his girlfriend. Just someone he knew."

"Cynthia, let him go. He has some great lessons to learn."

We finished our conversation.

I dialed Jen. "Hi, Jen."

"Cin, are you okay? I haven't heard from you in a long while."

"Sorry, I'm losing it."

I didn't want to unload any more of this craziness on Jen. I was sounding like a broken record.

"Margaret tells me to let him break up."

"Margaret is right. Cin, this clearly is a blessing in disguise."

"The disguise. Oh yes, *de olé* disguise," I commented, disheartened.

"I know, it's hard for you right now, but just imagine…the next poor woman who comes into his life—"

I interrupted, "I honestly cannot speculate about anyone else right now as I'm having a tough time."

I changed the subject, and we ended our conversation.

Monday came along and I had to ask Randy for help that evening. I clearly didn't want to, but there was no one else who lived close. He came by and stayed an hour, kissed me on the cheek, and left. The very next day, my car kept dying as I was out and about. I needed more assistance from Randy. I called to see if he could meet me at the mechanic's shop since my car needed to be inspected. He said he'd bring me back to his place to wait for my car; it wasn't too far from where he lived. I patiently stood outside waiting at the mechanic's. Randy drove up and got out of his car and, as he stepped closer, I noticed he was wearing the same clothes as the night before. As he reached for my cheek to kiss me, I cringed with disbelief.

I looked at Randy with sorrow. *Is he for real? He didn't even have the common courtesy to change clothes? Am I seeing this situation correctly? I'm leading such a dysfunctional life. Dear God, help me. Help me to get out of this in one piece!*

Disoriented, I pulled back, almost hyperventilating. I had to start taking deep, slow breaths so I could get through this disrespectful situation. I wanted to run away!

We reached Randy's place. I asked to go to the bathroom. I had to remove myself from what I had just witnessed and splash water on my face to help me get a grip. I passed his bedroom; his bed was made. Unfolded clean laundry was tossed all over it. He never makes his bed. The cleaning people make it. They were there yesterday. Today is today. Last night was last night.

I barely walked back from the restroom and pleaded for strength to face this man who was now like a stranger. I pretended to listen to his small talk, but I couldn't hear anything. My thoughts questioned the things he had done for me. I needed to get out of there as the walls were closing in. Just when I thought of this idea, the mechanic called and said my car was ready.

Randy drove back to my car and left. The mechanic made it a point to talk to me as I was heading for the office to pay my car repair bill.

"Cynthia, I found nothing wrong with your car."

"That's interesting. It kept stalling. Can I get in tomorrow if it occurs again?" I was totally confused.

"Sure."

I paid my bill, got into my car, and drove home numb. I couldn't sleep the entire night.

22: Angels and the Massage Oil Potion

I called Margaret the next day.

"Hi, Margaret. I'm falling apart again." I told her the latest.

"Darling, I know it's difficult. The good news, your time with him is almost complete. And the angels have guided you to all that you've found out!"

"Margaret, the angels, who I want to fire, have guided me to this dysfunctional situation! I think they fiddled with my car so I would call Randy to pick me up!"

"I wouldn't be surprised. Cynthia, remember the raccoons you ran into at the garbage area? This was the first sign. What did your book say about raccoons? Well, the mask is coming off, isn't it?"

"Yes, I guess so. I'm so burned out, Margaret. Here's one for the relationship history books!"

"Cynthia, are you meditating?"

"Not as much as I should, Margaret."

"It will soon be over. You need to let him break up with you. He has a bit of a temper, doesn't he?"

"Yes, the temper. I don't know how much more I can take, Margaret."

"I'm here if you need me. Love you."

"Love you too, Margaret. Goodbye."

I decided to sit and meditate to settle down. After a half hour, I calmed down but all of a sudden I heard, "Cynthia, you must go to his home; there is something left for you to do."

Huh? Am I hearing this correctly?

"Go to his home; you have a key. It's necessary."

It's necessary? I felt pushed once again. I got up, called Randy's work phone. He answered, so I asked something unimportant, and that was the end of that. I picked up my purse, scooped up the keys with his house key attached, and noticed the wand sitting there. Oh, what the heck! I picked it up and nervously drove to his home thinking someone might catch me. I didn't know how to act since sneaking wasn't a specialty of mine. I was shaking while I unlocked the front door. I stomped to his bedroom. There was laundry on the bed, and the sheets looked as though they were…um…stained with…

I examined closely and thought, *is it massage oil?* I opened the drawer on the side of the bed where he kept "our massage oil." Our oil was almost to the back of the drawer. There was a brand new oil with a little missing from the bottle.

"Is this what you wanted me to find?" I asked my angels out loud.

I shut the drawer. I began walking away with the new oil in hand, mumbling curse words to myself, when I accidentally kicked something under the bed. I bent down and picked up a book *Kama Sutra*. I thumbed through it. As I turned to various pages, I could see that the book showed lots of sexual positions. I was now beside myself. I rushed out of his home, locked the door, ran to the car, and screamed all the way home!

For some reason, my weary eyes zoomed in on the massage oil

on the seat. There appeared to be a smiling face looking at me. I thought to myself, *I'm going insane for sure.* I picked it up and realized it was a silhouette of oil stain on the bottle. *A smiling face?* I wanted to throw it out the window of the car, but then an idea jumped into my head. I began talking to myself.

"Okay, Randy boy, you want to play around, I'm going to make a special potion and add it to the new massage oil."

I stepped on the gas, turned up the music, and began singing. I picked up my magic wand, danced in my seat, and poked the wand here and there. Feeling bold, I rolled down the window and pointed the wand toward the sky.

I parked the car and darted towards the kitchen, put the massage oil on my counter with the wand, and began looking through my cupboards. I then thought, *Hmmm, let me make this a grand occasion!* I strutted into my bedroom to my walk-in closet and searched for the gown, took it off the hanger, and held it up high off the ground, never imagining I would be wearing it during a circumstance like this. I unzipped the back, slipped it on, and dubiously stared in the mirror, almost crying. I searched for the tiara in a drawer and placed it on my head

I walked over to the kitchen cupboard where all of my seasonings were and began slowly dropping in crushed red pepper as I danced around my kitchen. Then I added peppermint and a little white vinegar. I shook the bottle to see if it was abnormal looking. *Nope. Perfect!* I poured a glass of chardonnay and searched for my oldie CDs in the living room so I could dance some of the dances of my generation: the jerk, the swim, mash potatoes, and a new dance that just came to mind!

I began dancing the "jerk" and dedicated this dance to Randy.

"This one is for you, Randy!" My tiara fell off, but I placed it back on my head. I then started moving my arms to do the swim, talking to myself, "I'm almost drowning in this relationship." I held my nose tightly as I moved my other arm to swim and bent down to the ground. I kept saying to myself, "Cin, don't sink. Don't sink. You'll make it! You'll make it!"

Now, the mashed potato. "This is how my brain and heart feels right now, mashed."

I went back to the kitchen and grabbed the bottle of chardonnay, my full glass, and wand and plopped on the couch. I took a few sips, and yelled and screamed to the universe while holding my wand pointed to the ceiling. I screamed, "Angels, what were you thinking?" and took a few more sips of wine and pointed again to the ceiling.

"Why did you put a man like this in my life? Is this the *karma* Margaret talked about?"

All of a sudden the phone rang. I stopped my rant. I eyed the phone, got up, and ran to look at the caller ID. I froze. It was Randy. The phone looked like it was vibrating. Or was it the wine affecting me? Or the dancing? I turned off the music, answered, and tried to maintain and comprehend what Randy was saying, but I was half looped after my one and a half glass limit.

Randy was whispering, "Cin, I'm not feeling well. I'm going to go to bed early. I'll talk to you tomorrow. Good night." He quickly hung up before I said goodnight.

I said to myself, "Something is up. He's whispering? I'm going to his house!"

I waited forty-five minutes to come down off the wine, ate a quick snack, and ran out the door to go to his home. I had this impulsive thought that I needed to bring my magic wand. I turned around and went back to get it. I jumped in the car, threw the wand on the passenger seat, and drove over to Randy's home in a frantic state.

As I was driving down a side street, I rolled my window down and pointed the wand out and up to the universe, "What are the reasons you are doing this to me?"

I got to the gate and put in the code, but it didn't work.

I keyed in the code again. No luck. I waited for another car to open it. It didn't take long. I sped in, parked the car away from his home, got out of my car with the wand in hand, and walked over to his car. I felt the hood. Randy's car was still warm after forty-five minutes? Maybe he wasn't home when he called? I went to the front door, with the wand in one hand and key in the other. I was ready to open the door without warning.

Then awful things went through my head. *What if this? What if that?* Briefly, my erratic thoughts went straight to the wand. *Why in the world did I bring this? I'm definitely losing it!* I took a breath, too fearful to open the door, and decided to walk around to the master bedroom area on the side of his home to snoop and see if anything was going on there.

As I warily crept up to the bedroom, there was candlelight flickering through the crack in the wood blinds. I took a seat to wait under the window and placed the wand up against the wall of the home. Ten minutes later I heard laughter, sweet mumbling, and then moaning… I was totally grossed out. I wobbled away and was inching toward my car when I remembered the wand that I had left against the wall.

"Oh my God. I forgot the wand!"

I crawled back, almost on my hands and knees, picked up the wand, and ran back to the car. I began to get dizzy and felt as if I was going to throw up. I held on to the car, stooped over, and vomited. I got into my car and searched for a Kleenex as I was a mess.

Again, I reviewed everything that transpired as I was wiping my mouth. *Am I nuts and he's sane? Or, is he intentionally making me nuts?* I threw the wand in the back seat and drove home. I was still dizzy, holding my head with my hand leaned up against the car window. I was totally disgusted. I parked the car, unsteadily stammered to my home, unlocked the door, and aimed for my bedroom. I threw my dreary self on my bed, cried, fell fast asleep in my clothes, and dreamt about a play scene in Paris.

* * *

I was sitting in the audience, close to the front, at a sold-out play. The leading actor blissfully danced as he moved across the stage, captivating everyone in the theater. His English accent was music to the Parisian's ears, and to mine in particular. I could not take my eyes off him. Women made up the bulk of the audience, smitten and longtime followers of the leading English man. I made it a point to attend every play he brought to Paris and, affected as I was, I had fancied some kind of connection between us. But this evening, as he belted out an unforgettable beautiful song, our eyes met. I don't know if it was for a second or a century, but that moment—our eyes staring into each other's souls—was enough for me to know. I knew him.

Awhile later I was strolling through the outdoor market, gathering vegetables, when I felt it, like a warmth surging through me. He was nearby. Before I had a chance to turn, I felt a gloved hand upon mine. Taking a deep breath, I raised my eyes and met his.

"Madam, may I?" he asked, relieving me of my half-filled basket. I gladly handed him the woven basket. He paid the clerk, and we walked slowly away from the market toward the peacefulness of the river. I had to keep my eyes away from his because when we made eye contact, I would almost forget my own name. I noticed his shoes, which were two-toned and were oddly familiar.

Our courtship began immediately and we eventually married. He was charming and comical. He became madly and confidently in love with me. Something in my reserved nature must've made him feel the need to prove it, because at every turn he was proclaiming his undying love. He would take me in his strong arms, dance, and sing sweet love songs. One day he yelled my name from the top of the Eiffel Tower and announced his love for me on the steps of Mount Mart. I never doubted him, and he never doubted me. We were inconsolably in love with each other.

Then I became ill. Very ill. Our relationship had been a stable rock, and now the rock was crumbling. He wept and begged me not to leave him. He fed and bathed me and lingered by my side every hour of the day and night. He wouldn't accept any offers of assistance from my circle of family and friends. I lost my ability to move or speak, only able to stare at the world behind a mute mask. I focused on his beautiful eyes, his strong hands, and his passion and unconditional love for me. He continued to sing sweet love songs and dance around the room, offering a glimpse of hope and a reminder of our special connection. He remained dedicated to the every end. I died in his arms.

I woke to the phone ringing.

* * *

"Wow, what a story! True love!" I looked at the clock and noticed it was 9:23 the next morning.

9:23? Go away 23!

"Hello?" I answered, half asleep.

"Hi, Cynthia, this is Margaret. How are you, darling? I had a strong feeling that I must call you today."

"It's been very multifaceted ordeal, to say the least, Margaret. I was a naughty girl last night and did not remember my spiritual manners."

I went into the potion story.

Margaret started chuckling. "My, you're a creative person, Cynthia."

"Randy called while I was yelling at the universe once more. He was whispering that he was ill and going to bed early. Something just didn't feel right." I went on with the story.

"Oh dear."

"I parked myself under his bedroom window, Margaret. He had someone in his bed. Honestly, I don't want to review what I heard."

Margaret was then voiceless.

"I was afraid this was going to happen."

"Why didn't you tell me, Margaret, if you knew?"

"You must get through this lesson somewhat by yourself. It's necessary. There is a greater cause than you know right now. Please trust me on this one."

Now silence from me.

"Cynthia, darling, are you still there?" Margaret asked.

"Yes. Barely!" I started sobbing. "Here I go on a month-long retreat to Brazil. The most alive and grounded I've felt in a long while. I re-meet this guy from the '70s that I kept at arm's length for awhile, and now I know why! I feel I've regressed."

"Are you meditating?"

"It's been challenging." Sniff, sniff.

"Cynthia, this will help tremendously."

"Most often, I cannot get my mind to settle down. I'm too stirred up!"

"I understand, but this is the point of meditation, isn't it? I realize you feel that you've regressed. Brazil was definitely preparing you for your next step, and this is it! It's a difficult one, for sure."

"It's been such a bizarre experience. Who knows how long he's been dating, and maybe there's more than one! Then there's a few other people thrown in the mix that I'm not thrilled with either!"

"Please be patient, it will be over soon."

"Margaret, I just woke up from another unusual dream." I went into the detail of Paris, the actor, the love affair, me dying. Margaret listened intently as I went through each facet of the dream.

"And the strange part, he was wearing two-toned shoes."

"Extraordinary! Those shoes certainly get around, don't they?" said Margaret amusedly.

"Yes, it appears so."

"The man in the dream is Randy too. Each incarnation we have is unique. He probably has remnants he's brought forward, but he appears fragmented now."

"It feels like it to me as well," I responded in agreement.

"Even though that lifetime had the aspects of perfection in that relationship, a glimpse of heaven on earth, what were you actually learning? You could have remained in heaven to experience total perfection. Have you forgotten why you came here?" Margaret compassionately asked.

Margaret hushed me.

"We don't grow much when things are perfect, do we?"

"Perhaps I should have stayed in heaven. I would rather experience true love instead of all of this shit," I cried out, tired of the drama. I was stricken by a sudden wave of sadness. I wanted to go back to the dream, to the magical place before my illness. I was mesmerized by the unconditional love I received.

"You know, Margaret, it was very challenging to experience severe illness in that dream. Even though my part in this difficult lesson was different from his, we both felt devastated leaving each other. It was an awful feeling."

"Cin, we only leave our bodies behind. Our soul lives on forever."

"Yes, I understand that the souls who are connected are close at hand. At this juncture in my life and while I inhabit this body, it's not the same. I cannot feel a soul. How do you hug or kiss a soul, Margaret? Can they share a meal or intimately assist you in the chores of life? I want a connection that a human provides. Preferably, a wonderful man who has done his work with two feet deeply rooted and committed in the relationship. I want the closeness of human touch and emotions, sharing joys, the dilemmas, and figuring the complexity of life's puzzle together."

"Since we are having a human experience, a connection is necessary. However, as you advance spiritually, souls will play a vital role in your life, which will help you to move past the current restrictions."

I was so worn out that I didn't want to get into the depth of what Margaret was trying to convey. I felt like it was too much work to wrap my mind around, so I dropped the soul subject.

"In the dream, I was completely captivated by how this man was there for my every need to the very end of my life." I began crying. I realized no one in this life had ever adored me like that, ever. Doesn't everyone want that sort of connection? I realized, as a woman born in the '50s, we were taught to be the one to cater to our significant other. Now looking back, we were taught to be the caregivers to everyone. Our needs were secondary.

Margaret sensed that I didn't want to go much further and felt my emotion. "Cin, I realize this is a very difficult phase for you right now. You are and will be growing by leaps and bounds in the next few years. You will write about this experience to help others."

Margaret paused again. "And yes, unconditional love is our true nature. You call it adore. I call it unconditional."

"Margaret, I cannot even help myself." My voice was cracking while I reached for a Kleenex. I'm now remembering more of my childhood NDE; the Angels shared some scenes of me judging my father after episodes of rage. It was the first time I sensed that his violent behavior was not who he was. And then, Gertie also talked about some enlightening stories and wisdom on this subject.

Margaret was contemplating. "Yes, as hard as it was, there is a bigger plan."

Margaret continued. "Randy's definitely running from this relationship. Running from himself, really. Running away is about avoiding. Possibly, he does this a lot in his life. So, he cannot commit to any relationship, even if he's in one, or so it appears."

"I don't know what to think. My brain and heart are mush."

"Cynthia, the pain you are feeling is purposeful. It has little to do with Randy. The dream you had is very symbolic. This is your play, Cin. Randy is an actor performing a vital role to help you stretch and grow through the human experience. He's a very good actor at that. And remember, you planned this before you came down here. You made a soul contract."

"Academy award material for sure."

"It would make a good movie," Margaret added.

"All of what you conveyed, my mind understands the concept, Margaret. But my heart has some catching up to do!"

Margaret agreed, "It may not be what you want right now, but it's what you need. Years from now you'll look back at this differently. Dear, I must go and tend to Gerald. I'll light a candle and pray for you. Bye for now. Love you."

"Love you too, Margaret. Thank you!"

I got off the phone; my feelings were worn to the bone again! Pain had been a constant companion. Something I'd had more than enough of.

* * *

I had one last thing to do before this was over—return my beloved special potion massage oil! I called Randy's work and asked the receptionist if he was in.

"Yes, I'll connect you."

After a brief silence, his office phone rang. Under my breath I uttered, "No, you won't connect me. I've had enough connection with this man for many lifetimes!" I hung up, got dressed, and walked swiftly out the door with the massage oil in hand. I got to Randy's home and dialed the code. It didn't work again. "He changed the code. Oh well. I'll wait for a car to let me in," I muttered out loud. I then thought about the other evening when I tried to enter the code a few times with no luck.

What I was about to do wasn't spiritual, but I was not in a spiritual mood. I was disappointed with my angels and at my wit's end!

Two cars drove up back-to-back and I eased in. I swiftly got out of the car, slammed the door, and walked a few steps, forgetting the potion. So I walked back, collected it, shut the door, and got to his front door looking around as I was unlocking it. I tiptoed to his bedroom. Why I tip toed? Who knows? I was off my rocker now.

The bed was unmade. Clothes were everywhere. I opened the nightstand drawer next to his bed and peeked inside. The old massage oil wasn't there. I felt the back of the drawer with my hand and there it was. It was almost empty.

"So, he used it the other night?" I said out loud.

I tossed the new massage oil in the drawer, closed it, and walked quickly out the front door, locked it, and got in my car. I cranked the music, took a few deep breaths, and let go of everything while I sang to the song playing on the radio.

The next day I asked Randy to come over. I confronted him with some of the evidence. He denied everything and said that I was imagining things and that he was going to take a mental health break and come back to talk.

I remembered Margaret stressing to let Randy break up. This was so difficult because I wanted to let him have it with both barrels.

I went to the couch to meditate, and my neck began hurting. I started to massage to relax the tight muscles and I began reminiscing about Brazil since the massage triggered a memory.

23: Trust, Faith, and Total Belief

I remember sitting outside of the posada, half interested in a book, lounging in front of my room. I began chatting with my neighbor and asked if she knew of a massage therapist. One of the reasons I went to Brazil was to heal an old, troublesome neck injury from a car accident. She mentioned this Irish Hare Krishna man, named Arden. He was the massage therapist for John of God and gave fabulous massages. Arden was described as a short, bald man, with reddish facial hair, in Hare Krishna clothing. I asked where I could find him. She expressed to just put the thought out there and he would show up.

Is she serious? Put the thought out there and he'll show up? This was 2001. I wasn't into such things, but I was curious to learn more.

I thought about Arden the following days as I walked the dusty dirt roads of Abadiania. One specific day, after The Casa session, I thought I recognized the profile I was given. This short, bald man with reddish facial hair and a Hare Krishna outfit was walking down the same path, joyfully whistling. To me, he resembled a leprechaun. As we walked close enough, I stopped.

"Hello, are you a massage therapist?"

"Yes, indeed! At your service!"

I smiled and made an appointment right on the spot.

The very next day, I walked down to Arden's posada and knocked on his door for my massage. He answered in a jovial manner, inviting me in. Arden explained his massage approach and casually mentioned it was a donation type of payment. In the States, asking for a donation for a service was and is still unheard of. He gazed deeply into my eyes while talking and said, "Your eyes remind me of my lovely mother who passed away when I was a child." Tears welled up in Arden's eyes; he turned away as he was so taken by this experience.

Arden gathered his emotions, pointed me to an area to change, and he stepped outside. I hurriedly took off my street clothes, hopped up on the table, placed the worn, white sheet over me and waited. I quickly reviewed what Arden had just mentioned about his mother. As I lay on the massage table, Arden walked up and began working the kinks out of my tight, aching neck. He was silent for awhile, honoring the quiet zone rule. I thought just maybe I could get him to open up.

"Arden, do you feel comfortable sharing more about your mother?"

I waited. He remained questionably reserved.

For a few seconds I thought that maybe I had overstepped boundaries. More silence. Arden kept massaging, but the pressure of his touch shifted as if he was in deep thought.

"Cynthia, I've kept my feelings inside."

"Arden, do you feel this is healthy?"

"No."

I chose my words carefully; I felt this opportunity could be a tiny, lighted opening for Arden. "If you feel safe, I'm here to listen."

More quietness. Suddenly, I intuitively knew he was trying to find a way to purge. I sensed a memory percolating. Arden's voice cracked with emotion with an uneven pitch. He cleared his throat.

"After my mother's death, I was a very lonely child, yearning for a stabilizing and nurturing female figure. As far back as I can remember, in childhood and even into my teenage years, I would stand back and study the ways of my friends' mothers. How their mothers interacted and nurtured them. How their mothers were supportive during all the important events in their lives. What was one of the most difficult moments, though, was when I was ill with the mumps one year. I begged God to bring my mother back. I needed her love, her special touch. I cried many nights alone. I suffered in silence for too long and wondered if the deep engrained pain would ever subside. Unfortunately, the closest I ever got to a mother figure was just observing these women. I was too timid to ask, and they never offered."

I wrapped the white drape around me, sat up, and turned to Arden to emotionally comfort him. "Arden, I feel your pain, and I'm so sorry this happened. I feel there were reasons for your loss and now, the answers are not far away. Your father, he couldn't be there for you?"

Arden restlessly turned away, not wanting me to witness his vulnerability. He composed himself. "My father was in his own grief and handled it privately as most men did those days. So, this is how my siblings and I managed our distress, privately. It's been locked away until now."

I felt Arden's torment. I was tearing up now, picturing Arden as a grieving child, without a mother, but then, I carefully observed that the afflicted child was still somewhere inside, pleading for healing. Arden noticed my innate reaction. This triggered a stream of tears within him. He politely excused himself and left the sparse room.

I waited and attentively watched the door. Arden returned minutes later, red-eyed but composed.

"Arden, are you okay?"

"Yes, I feel better, Cynthia. Thank you."

I felt honored that Arden had bestowed a gift of trust in me. I hoped this purging helped him to begin the long awaited process to mend a part of his life that was probably his next step on his soul journey. I sensed that Arden's mother had a hand in our meeting, and I told him so. He smiled and let out a deep sigh, as if this was finally the miracle required to begin healing. We moved on to other subjects while Arden resumed the massage, and then he fondly talked about his nomadic life on the road, which simply amazed me. It was as if he was called to places on short notice, following his intuition. His roots were very Irish, but his sense of adventure took him all over the world. It sounded like he loved being portable. Actually, his life was more alluring than mine at that point, but little did I know, it was about to dramatically change!

Finally, at the end of our visit, Arden also mentioned that he had been in Brazil for several months and needed funds to go on a pilgrimage to India soon. He conveyed that he had no money so far and was praying to God for the funds. Arden needed the equivalent of $3,000. "God will provide," Arden assuredly responded.

I intently listened.

Arden said that if he desired anything or needed to be somewhere, he would pray for it and believed it would arrive. I was taken aback by his faith, trust, and complete knowing that God would provide. Interestingly, according to Arden, God always provided whatever he asked for.

My curiosity was piqued.

The massage was two hours long. He worked magic on my neck. I had no idea what to give him since the donation concept was new to me. What I gave, he humbly appreciated. As I was walking out the door, Arden mentioned the fact that he was in total trust and faith, and he would get the funds needed to go to India. Arden faintly smiled while watching my reaction and keenly understood I had trouble believing.

We hugged. Arden broke loose and gazed straight into my eyes, holding each of my arms in his hands. Undeniably, it was vital to get what he was about to say.

"Cynthia, you must learn to have faith and trust too!"

I affectionately smiled but felt uncertain about this request. I contemplated what he was asking God for. I went to Abadiania not only to get healing for an old neck injury, but to also get needed rest. I hoped to find the answers I was seeking through lots of prayer and meditation—but most importantly, to be led to the next step in my life. Arden presented a new, huge lesson that I had never expected, which was something I should have been incorporating to move forward.

I left in deep thought.

Brazil is a third-world country. Poverty appeared everywhere, especially Abadiania. *How could Arden get this kind of money in the desired time frame in which he expected it?* I mentioned the story to a few people the following day. They too were very interested in Arden's request to God. *The Secret*, a concept introduced by Rhonda Byrnes, wasn't even a clever thought in her mind yet.

About three days past. While walking with a few farm animals on one of the dirt roads in Abadiania, I heard someone calling my name.

"Cyn-th-ia, Cyn-th-ia." I looked around but didn't see anyone. I kept walking. Out of nowhere, Arden materialized.

"Cynthia, I've been searching all over for you! I want to tell you

I'm going to India soon. I have the funds I prayed for."

"What? It's only been three days."

Arden pulled out a huge wad of rolled-up money from his shirt pocket and said that someone just magically showed up for a massage and gifted him with all the funds he needed for India. His eyes twinkled with delight.

I was speechless and took a breath.

"Arden, did you mention your trip to India to the very generous person?" I asked, in a curious manner.

"No."

"No?" After this gripping news, I hugged Arden and was happy his prayers were answered. We conversed awhile more and he went off whistling, disappearing in a flash.

I began walking to my posada, talking to God.

"Okay, God, I know this lesson is for me."

What I had just experienced with Arden gave me a push of motivation to review my life and question the many years when I'd lacked trust, faith, and total belief.

"Ask and you'll receive. Ask and you'll receive. What an incredible lesson and teacher you put before me! Thank you, God and angels!"

Arden remarkably showed up in my life. It truly was the right time and place. I continued to thank God for steering Arden to me. Even to this day, I'm in deep gratitude for the privilege of his presence and the useful life lesson. I wanted to keep in contact with Arden and tried for months to locate him through others I had met in Abadiania. But

Arden vanished without a trace.

I was almost to my posada, but I decided to walk down to The Casa to meditate in the main meeting area. The sun was beginning to set; there was just a little light left in one corner of the room. There were a few people scattered about, each in prayer or meditation. I sat down and noticed a woman who was one of my neighbors at the posada. She recognized me, and we both smiled and waved to each other. I began taking some deep breaths to relax. I needed my mind to settle. On the fourth breath, as my eyes faced forward, something whisked into the room. It swirled around and around, and then disappeared. I wanted to jump up with excitement. I eagerly glanced at my neighbor and she acknowledged the sighting.

"Did you see that?" I asked.

She grinned, "Yes, what was it?"

"I feel it's one of the entities," I eagerly responded.

She agreed, nodding her head up and down.

We both settled down from this unique experience and got into a quiet meditative state. After awhile it seemed like I had left my body. It was as if I was on top of the Universe. I'd never felt this before.

I walked back to the posada and retired early. The next morning I awoke late and had twenty minutes to make the morning meditation. I threw on some white clothing, washed my face, brushed my teeth, and combed and rubber banded my hair up and back. I quickly grabbed my rosary, which was from Fatima, Portugal, off of the wooden shelf and the burlap bag that had the things I needed for the day. As I fumbled, I tangled the rosary on the handle of the woven bag. I tried to unscramble it, but I made more of a mess. I let it be and rushed over to the dining hall for a quick breakfast. I gobbled down an egg and toast and walked the dirt path in haste toward The Casa. In a frustrated manner, I glanced at the rosary and thought I'd try once more to unsnarl it, but now it was twisted and hooked up in too many places. I impatiently gave up as I entered the meditation area.

I placed my sack under the long bench in front of me and stared at the mangled rosary, shaking my head in disbelief. I wanted to devotedly hold onto it because this blessed rosary had been my traveling companion all over the world—placed on holy altars, taken to sacred mountain tops, held closely while quietly meditating in a dark cave with a monk at a gathering. I had blessed the rosewood rosary further by dipping it in the holy water angel bowl at Fatima, Portugal, and set it by the candles lit by pilgrims. Numerous life events it was placed in the hands of those who for some reason appeared. Some inquisitively watched and inquired as to why I held onto something that only Catholics have made holy. When I went into the astonishing stories, countless people would want to hold the rosary as if perhaps Our Lady would appear and answer their prayers. Now, it's here with me at The Casa in Abadiania, tangled on my bag, but thoughts of it absorbing the love and energy of the sacred meditation room gently calmed my feelings quickly. I slowly closed my eyes and sat there for three hours, barely moving. Suddenly, it was announced that meditation was over. I bent down to pick up my burlap bag and noticed the rosary laying neatly over it. I couldn't believe my eyes. I picked up my bag and rosary and briskly walked out to look for my friend Sal. I noticed he was sitting outside on one of the carved wooden benches gazing out into the scenic valley.

"Sal, I just had a wild paranormal experience!" I began sharing the rosary story.

"That's crazy! Are you sure you didn't just place the rosary on your bag and forget the position?"

"You're not listening. The rosary was all tangled. Look. See how each section has these wire pieces. Look how they can hook together," I was frustrated that Sal didn't believe me. I witnessed a supernatural anomaly, but he wouldn't have it.

"Well, I don't know about this. It sounds awfully weird."

I dropped the subject when a couple walked up to chat.

The next morning, I sat in my small room meditating before breakfast. I was confused and asked myself if tangling the rosary was something I should be doing. I waited for some sort of guidance.

Cynthia, this rosary is symbolic to you. Those who don't believe in such things don't have a strong opinion one way or another. They would be more curious to find out what happened next. Those who are Catholic may feel you're being disrespectful, but are you really?

I was torn after the fact.

I then felt a knot in the pit of my stomach. I began to consider, "What if this miracle was a one-time occurrence?" I started reminiscing and remembering all the journeys this gift had been on, but this was something I never experienced before, and I wanted to explore this phenomenon more. I decided to tangle the rosary. I put myself together and walked over to the dining hall to have breakfast. Sal was already there. I placed my bag on the chair next to him and stood in the small breakfast buffet line. I energetically walked back and set my plate down, sat, and began eating.

"I see your rosary is tangled. You did this intentionally?" Sal half joked as he observed my burlap bag.

187

"Yes, I want to see if this miracle will occur again."

"You're serious?" Sal was half curious and half not believing.

"We will see, won't we?"

"I guess," Sal quickly responded and changed the subject.

It was time for us to get on our way to the morning meditation. We briskly strode down the dusty path with dozens of foreigners dressed in all white attire, steadily heading for The Casa.

As we took our seats, I placed my burlap bag once more under the long bench in front of me. I touched the rosary in a few places to make sure it was ready to face whoever was playing with me.

Three hours went by. The facilitators announced the ending of the meditation. I opened my eyes and peered at my bag. My rosary was lying neatly over my bag, just like before. I jumped up rapidly and turned to Sal to show him.

"No way! Cin, I just don't believe this. Maybe someone took your bag and untangled the rosary," Sal was very clear in assessing the situation.

"Sal, no one moved from the meditative position the entire session. What more proof do you need?" I was almost beside myself since my friend was still questioning this miraculous occurrence. I stepped back and immediately stopped my judgment.

"I got to go find Margaret," I quickly commented. I gave Sal a hug and off I went looking for Margaret.

I hurriedly walked down the dirt road back into the sleepy little village and noticed Margaret having lunch with a twenty-something young man. I strolled over excitedly and uttered, "Margaret, something far out just happened!" I caught and excused myself for barging in. "I'm sorry. I'm so excited I forgot my manners."

"Dear, no worries. Please sit down. This is Justin."

"Hello, Justin. So sorry for my rudeness."

"No apologies are necessary. Now, tell us your news." Justin was very intrigued to possibly hear another magical story since Abadiania was filled with them.

I proceeded to express the details of the rosary miracle with Margaret and Justin. Both were puzzled since this was not a story Margaret or Justin had heard before. This was Margaret's eighth visit to Abadania and has a plethora of stories she could detail for weeks. This odd experience was new.

"Cin, I've not heard of anything like this."

"Honestly?" I sat in fascination.

"I've been here for over three months and no one has ever mentioned anything remotely close to this occurrence," Justin politely added.

"Wow," was all I could say after hearing Margaret and Justin.

We went on to other subjects, and I then excused myself. I suddenly felt tired and went back to the posada to take a much-needed nap. That evening I met up with Sal in the dining area. I placed my bag on the arm of the chair once again and lined up for dinner. I noticed Sal hunting for my rosary on my bag and following me to the buffet line.

"Where's the rosary?"

"In my bag," I smiled and responded.

"The tangled rosary on your bag got untangled again?"

"Yes."

I dished my meal and maneuvered through the crowded room. I didn't pursue the rosary story, mainly because this was too wild for Sal to comprehend.

We chit chatted about the day and finished our meal. I walked back to my room, grabbed a book to read, dilly dallied to the lush garden, and took a seat on an inviting bench. I immediately thought about the next day. It would be my last whole day at The Casa.

Should I tangle the rosary one last time?

I laid the book on the bench beside me and closed my eyes to meditate. After a half hour, some enlightening messages emerged. I released my frustration about Sal's reaction and knew he was in a place he needed to be, and I accepted it with no more judgment. After all, this was an off-the-wall situation. I took a deep breath, picked up my book, and began reading.

The next morning, I sat at the edge of my unmade bed with the rosary in hand. *Should I attempt this once more?* I said to myself.

"Please angels, give me a confirmation that I will be able to untangle the rosary if the spirits decide not to participate today."

Just then my phone alarm went off. Mesmerizing, since I hadn't set my phone alarm.

I intricately began to tangle my rosary. Again, I had that awful feeling. At a confused state, butterflies noisily floated around in my stomach. Was it guilt I was feeling? Guilt was something I'd been working on the last few years. It was tough to overcome given that it was embedded since childhood. It's been a part of the human race and religions for too long. After the guilt feeling dissipated, I knew I'd find a way.

Sal wasn't around during breakfast. I finished my meal and left. When I got to the meditative area of The Casa, I followed the same routine of placing my bag under one of the long benches in front of me and touching the rosary to make sure it was ready for the playful spirit.

After four hours of meditation, I opened my eyes just a tad and examined the place on my bag where the discombobulated rosary held itself. There it was, a perfect mess. *All tangled.* My back was beginning to ache, so I moved around and thought another position would help, but no avail. After the fifth hour, I had enough meditation and again peeked past my eyelashes only to find that the rosary was still in complete disarray.

Well, twice is enough. And now I needed the patience to untangle it, dear Lord!

Five minutes went by. The meditation leader announced that the session had ended. Everyone was more than relieved. I had never meditated that long before, ever. I reached for my bag. My rosary was lying across, untangled, in a different position altogether. I almost came unglued.

"Five minutes? It took them, him, her or it, five minutes to do this?" I said out loud, not worrying whether those standing around would presume I was crazy.

I went looking for Margaret. Sal wasn't interested, and I didn't want to waste my miracle excitement. Margaret knew these sorts of mystical occurrences were possible since she'd had some of her own.

If this could happen in five minutes, I figured anything was possible, such as the healings and cures that took place in Abadiania. In fact, as I thought about it, I realized that these sorts of miracles were instantaneous in many cases. How many people traveled to this special place on a wing and a prayer, after they tried absolutely everything that allopathic medicine failed to cure. How exciting it was to be able to hear and then observe the miracles.

24: The Dance of Forgiveness

I snapped out of my day dream. I found myself parked in front of my home, but couldn't remember getting there.-I was smiling from ear to ear, remembering my visit with Arden and the Fatima rosary story. It was a nice break from the craziness of the lesson I was now experiencing!

I vowed to get back to meditation—especially now— I also realized that I'd not followed Arden's teaching. I remembered one of the reasons I went to Brazil: to find out what my next step was. I wasn't happy with myself since I hadn't been specific and was now in a fix.

I needed faith, trust, and belief that this drama had to occur for greater reasons. But, at this crossroad, I was clueless what the greater reasons were.

One thing was for sure: I received a doozy!

I walked in the house to the phone ringing. I ran over to answer it.

"Hi, Cin. What's going on? I haven't heard from you and wanted to see how you were?"

"Hi, Jen. There's so much to unload. I'll fill you in on the latest, and then I got to run." I went over the story of how I went to Randy's home, listened to all the noise, and almost left the wand under the window outside of his bedroom.

"Unbelievable!" Jen was belly laughing!

"Yes, isn't it?" I stated in a serious tone. "Jen, I've spent way too much energy on this ordeal. I'm sure your ear is red and sore like

Margaret's. Let's move on. I'm done! How are you?" I hurriedly asked, wanting to change the subject.

We chatted for a little while more, and then I had to rush off to do an errand. Afterwards, I decided to take a much-needed walk in the woods to get back into nature. I drove to a serene, secluded park outside of town. On the way, I was listening to Judy Collins singing a Bob Dillon song *Blowin' in the Wind.* I began singing this old, favorite song and remembered a Judy Collins concert I had watched with an old Bellarmine Prep boyfriend, back in high school, while I was attending Presentation High School, an all-girls college prep school, early in the '70s.

I began going back in memory to one of the Bellarmine mixers where I had first met Luke. Immediately, I felt a connection as he strutted up to me and my friend and asked me to dance. Luke was a moose. His hands were double the size of mine. I knew right away that Luke was a football player and a good one at that. This began a six-month steady relationship, the kind girls keep a scrapbook filled with mementos—the ones with newspaper clippings of newsworthy sports events, corsages, concert and event stubs, and photos. Our short relationship together almost filled an entire scrapbook that my mother kept with all the other teen mementos and gave to me long after my marriage and divorce.

At our six-month anniversary, the relationship abruptly ended the night we took a stroll on a golf course behind his friend's parents' home. The stroll began with a kiss and then a make-out session, which was very common for teens in the '70s, rolling and tossing around, until the moment arrived when I refused to have sex with Luke. The breakup hurt a lot; I didn't understand that this would be a deal breaker. Disconcerting predicaments like this should be sorted out, but it wasn't meant to be. I never heard from Luke again. I was true to myself, and this is all that mattered.

The teenage disappointment eventually went away when I finally surfaced from under my sorrow and surprisingly noticed there were many fish in the sea. It was obvious that I needed to learn more about relationships considering the universe provided a variety of young men who were interested. More than I imagined. I still stayed true to myself since I wasn't ready to surrender to anyone.

I stopped the reminiscing and began singing this song Judy Collins made popular.

I parked and meandered to one of the winding trails in front of me. I had many questions, and maybe the long awaited answers were blowing in the wind. At times, I missed something significant, yet so simple to those evolved.

Lately, I had a one-dimensional focus, and felt stagnated. After a half hour of walking, no answers came. I thought, *Enough of drowning in the adversity.* I wanted relief from the drama and welcomed the feeling of being in arms of the wind and nature.

I took a seat and allowed the wind to hold and caress my aching heart, exhausted mind, and body. I finally took the time to look up at the sky and thanked God for this precious moment. Thoughts would come into my mind, but I would push them aside since I wanted to just be without the chatter. Briefly, I was given a sense of peace I had somehow lost. I was grateful. I never imagined that the wind could wrap me in its arms, but perhaps it was always there waiting for the day when I would wake up to this blessing. And just maybe this was the beginning of waking up from a slumber that had more challenges than benefits.

I drove home refreshed—ready for the end of this craziness.

Randy called a few days later and wanted to come over to talk. I knew this was the end. I was prepared, I thought. My angels and Margaret reminded me over and over, "There's more work to do, let him go."

I realized I had my own work to do and that this was best for both of us. The doorbell rang. He walked in. He was reserved and to the point.

"Here is your key. I wish you the best."

I took his key off my key chain, handed his to him, and that minute I thought about the potion. I chuckled to myself. I led him to the door and he was gone.

I waited about fifteen minutes. I began getting stirred up and then furious! I don't know what came over me. Maybe it was the accumulation of everything.

I drove over to his home and waited for another car to let me in. I knocked on the door, he answered, and I barged in while he had the phone glued to his ear. He was happy, laughing, and probably talking to whomever it was that was replacing me.

"Happy and laughing?"

I asked Randy to get off of the phone. I marched into each room, and began taking our photographs out of the frames that I had given to him and ripped the photos apart! He observed with no expression. With determined effort, I walked to the front door, opened it, and left. He was close behind. I turned, caught his elusive eyes, and said, "Who are you?"

He blankly stared and said nothing.

I walked away not believing what I had just done. As I was driving home, I began tearing up. I apologized to my angels.

"I'm sorry I've yelled, cried, pointed the wand, and wanted to fire you. I avoided my spiritual reasoning and behavior. Please forgive me."

That night was the best night's rest I'd had in awhile. It was a few days before my birthday and three weeks before Christmas. I spent my free time in bed recuperating.

One morning I woke up feeling like something was terribly wrong. I ran to the bathroom and began hemorrhaging. I had never done this before and got a bit frightened. I quickly prepared a make-shift feminine pad with a hand towel; the situation was overwhelming. I rushed myself to the hospital, saying out loud, "Happy birthday and merry Christmas, Cynthia!"

This topped off one of the most inconceivable experiences of my life! I was placed on meds to control the bleeding. It subsided and so did my erratic feelings for Randy.

One night while sleeping, I had one last dream regarding this stage of my life. I was taken back to Georgia again, to the charming lake where I had felt a sense of peace and solace. But now it was the present day. I was sitting there joyfully dazed, watching the birds and butterflies pass by, when I noticed a mirage of a woman walking toward me from across the way. As the woman approached she said, "Hello, Cynthia."

I eyed this woman intently as she ambled closer. The woman clearly realized I was confused.

"Gertie?" I squinted my eyes, trying to make sense of what was happening. "You don't look like Gertie, but it feels like you," I cautiously responded.

The woman cheerfully grinned. "Dear child, on the other side you know we become younger."

"Oh yes! I remember now!" I thought briefly of my near-death experience.

I examined Gertie, closely watching her mannerisms and listened attentively to her thick Austrian accent. It was now clear.

"My God, Gertie, it is you. I don't believe this is happening! What a miracle! I've felt your presence from time to time. And—my, oh my—all the synchronicities to connect Christi and me were incredible! And now, I can personally thank you for all the help you've provided through the years." I lovingly remembered the close parking spots. "And when I ask for assistance for parking, I'm continually in awe of your angelic capabilities, dedication, and service as my guardian angel. I miss you, Gertie."

Gertie affectionately smiled, Christi was having such a difficult time. She especially needed to experience these events as signs that I'm close by. She didn't get it right away like you. That was the only possible solution."

Gertie thoughtfully reflected. "I've heard and felt your thank yous and appreciation for my assistance through the years, Cynthia. Most humans have this idea that they need an image of a human body to feel like the communication has been heard."

Gertie half smiled and broke away into deep thought. She reached for her bunted-up hair, took a long strand from it, and began twirling it.

I watched in utter amazement. I opened my mouth a bit, and recollected our time while she was in the hospital. The habitual gesture was a tickling confirmation.

"Life has been very burdensome for you lately." Gertie gave me a comforting look.

I nodded with conviction, "Yes."

The tone of Gertie's voice was angelic in nature. There was a very luminous, white light surrounding her. The same radiant light I witnessed when I visited heaven as a child. The entire scene, surreal, almost brought me to tears. I sat in deep reverence while she continued.

"You're learning some great lessons about love right now, Cin. We realize how difficult this fated connection was for you."

I began looking back at the ordeal, took a deep breath, and then wondered about the "we" Gertie had just mentioned since there was no one else around. I then remembered all of my angels on the other side.

Gertie lovingly continued, taking her lock of hair and twisting it in a slow, hypnotic fashion as she stared at me in a persuasive manner.

"Cin, you've become lost. You've forgotten who you truly are."

I began tearing up. Gertie held the sacred space for the emotion I was feeling.

"It's all inside, Cin. It's all inside!" She paused again. "You know this. You've always known it's deep inside."

I had a soul-like remembrance, and my eyes lit up.

"You chose this penetrating hurt for a greater good. On this level of understanding, please remember, hurt is about wanting something different than what is. This is the suffering you feel. You had one idea, he had another."

"What do you mean *on this level of understanding*, Gertie?" I was puzzled.

"Remember our conversation in the hospital?"

"Which one? We had a few profound conversations." I was still unsure.

"The one about romantic love?" Gertie tenderly smiled and waited for my response.

"Oh yes."

"Again, true love is inside all of us. It doesn't come from out there! Most humans feel they need another to create this kind of love, and when it's supposedly gone, they blame the other." Gertie calmly waited for the light bulb to go on in my head.

"I didn't know about his hidden pattern until much later. He wasn't..." I stopped my ramble, caught myself going back to the drama, and refocused on Gertie.

Gertie gently stared at me with a compassionate heart. She instantly knew I was still stuck in the story. She understood that I wasn't ready to go deeper. I needed to heal before I could advance further.

"Cin, on the human level, he believes it's out there somewhere, like many others. He's running in circles. And you, you blame him for not being honest and are miffed how he led you down this untruthful path that ended in hurt. True, he wasn't forthcoming. But it boils down to the fact that he wasn't honest with himself. On this side, we view things differently. This experience presented an opportunity. It's not about the perception of right or wrong, spiritually speaking."

"Opportunity? How can this be an opportunity?" I asked puzzled.

"Ah-Ah-Ah. Once more, let's review. You see dear child, opportunity is in the lesson. It seems like you still don't remember the discussions in the hospital."

"I guess not."

Gertie could tell I was overwhelmed. "The teaching can be agonizing, or one can view it filled with purpose. But one must move through the pain and heal. Pain informs what one has not worked through. Hurt, anger, doubt, judgment, criticism—the list goes on. All are part of suffering and the learned human condition, which disconnects us from one's true nature and from each other," Gertie responded. "Once you heal from this experience, Cin, it will look and feel different. I promise."

"I hope so." I was so burned out. Painful remembering and learning was secondary.

"You've taken on this lesson to dramatically advance on the spiritual level of understanding. Remember, you have all the love you'll ever need inside. If you came from this belief, the experience would be a different story. You both have work to do. Before you can reach this advanced state, let's concentrate on the current story you're having extreme pain with."

Something finally clicked inside. I repeated to myself, *You have all the love you'll ever need inside.* I now felt Gertie opened a small crack of a jammed window leading into my heart.

Gertie gently observed, read my thoughts, and understood the importance of what this statement meant to me.

"The masks that humans sometimes wear, eventually come off."

"This one sure did!" I half-jokingly replied.

"We put the mischievous raccoons in your path," Gertie giggled as she continued to fidget with her long strand of hair.

"The raccoons? You put them in my path?"

"Yes," Gertie giggled again. "We knew you would take note. The *Animal Speak* book has been by your side for awhile."

I was in complete fascination.

"You were having car problems at one point?"

"Yes…"

"We tinkered a little with your car."

"You did? I thought so. I mentioned to Margaret that the angels had a hand in this."

"We deliberately moved this relationship along a little because we witnessed distressing things that you couldn't see."

I took a deep breath and drifted off again.

"And that potion, well, we cannot take total credit for that creation!" Gertie wanted me to smile to remain present.

Now I was the one giggling. Gertie grinned and tarried, enjoying the beautiful setting surrounding us.

"Some humans go looking here and then there, with this one or that one, or this material-find or that material-find. Each eventually disappoints. It's not somewhere outside. It's been inside all along, but most have forgotten."

I sat motionless.

"Your work isn't about him or any other. Let him go do what he needs to do. He has a plan like you."

"Focus on your own romantic dance, Cynthia. The dance of *you.*" Gertie stopped and studied my reaction. "What music will *you* play? Will it help you blossom into who you truly are?"

Gertie paused again, observing. She knew I was taking this in and wished that I would be able to bask in this life lesson. "Will you dance the dance of forgiveness?"

I thought about forgiveness and its lessons. I drifted off, watching the intricacies of nature—not concerned about human complexities, living in the moment and in joy. That's where I wanted to be—in joy. I asked myself how to get there.

"You have told others you've forgiven your father. Have you?"

I sat there wondering how Gertie knew this and then I again remembered her capabilities.

"I believe I have." I stated delicately.

"If you have forgiven your father on the deepest level, you'll in turn forgive Randy and any others who step into your world.

Gertie continued, "True love is the key to everything, Cin."

I turned my attention back to Gertie.

"Cin, remember who you are."

Gertie slowly got up, beaming. I followed her lead. She turned and gently held my hands. Her eyes were captivating, devotional, and limitless.

"Know that you are deeply loved."

We embraced.

"Goodbye for now, dear one. I'm as close as you want me to be."

Tears welled up in my eyes again. I didn't want to let her go. The invisible isn't the same as the physical. It was as if I was leaving heaven for the second time.

"Until we meet again. Goodbye, Gertie."

Gertie carefully broke loose from the cuddle, turned away, and began walking to where she had first appeared. She pivoted, looked back, slowly waved goodbye, and half yelled, "True love isn't a dress rehearsal…" Then she magically disappeared.

Somehow I didn't feel shattered anymore. I began moving my hips slowly to the romantic music that spontaneously began playing in my head. I had my arms and hands by my side and suddenly felt a silky material next to them. I focused downward and noticed that I was wearing the beautiful red gown Randy had bought for me. I began twirling and then waltzing, matching Gertie's steps slowly around the lake. I felt more alive than I had in awhile.

I began following my own music and danced my own unique dance. I left the red gown hanging up in my bedroom, on the edge of the door frame, for a few months as a reminder of the stages we must go through to get to a new understanding. Randy truly was the catalyst in this agonizing process.

From time to time, I've wondered how many red gowns are hanging, forgotten in closets, waiting to be worn for the next dance lesson in someone's life. It took awhile for me to heal from this ordeal. I finally realized that fate is different from destiny. Fate was the lesson. Destiny, the learned experience I made useful. The only true gift Randy gave to me was the opportunity to continue my journey- to love on the deepest level.

About the Author

Cynthia M. Long is a fifth generation Californian from the Silicon Valley Bay Area, now living in the Central Valley, who has been gifted with three adult children and three charming grandsons.

Cynthia has traveled the globe and spent a lifetime seeking out the unseen miracles of the spirit. Follow Cynthia as she begins recounting the many events and travels that continue to lead her to questioning whether love is a dress rehearsal on the dance floor of life.

A novella leading into "The Red Gown" adventure.